Life of William Grimes,
the Runaway Slave

Life of William Grimes, the Runaway Slave

Edited by

WILLIAM L. ANDREWS AND REGINA E. MASON

OXFORD
UNIVERSITY PRESS

2008

OXFORD
UNIVERSITY PRESS

Oxford University Press, Inc., publishes works that further
Oxford University's objective of excellence
in research, scholarship, and education.

Oxford   New York
Auckland   Bangkok   Bogotá   Buenos   Aires   Cape Town   Chennai
Dar es Salaam   Delhi   Hong Kong   Istanbul   Karachi   Kolkata
Kuala Lumpur   Madrid   Melbourne   Mexico City   Mumbai   Nairobi
São Paulo   Shanghai   Singapore   Taipei   Tokyo   Toronto

Copyright © 2008 by Oxford University Press

Published by Oxford University Press, Inc.
198 Madison Avenue, New York, New York, 10016

www.oup.com

Oxford is a registered trademark of Oxford University Press

Library of Congress Cataloging-in-Publication Data
Grimes, William, b. 1784.
Life of William Grimes, the runaway slave / edited by William L. Andrews
and Regina E. Mason.— Rev. ed.
p.   cm.
ISBN 978-0-19-534331-1; 978-0-19-534332-8 (pbk.)
1. Grimes, William, b. 1784.   2. Slaves—United States—Biography.
3. Fugitive slaves—United States—Biography.   4. Slaves—Virginia—King George
County—Biography.   5. African Americans—Connecticut—New Haven—Biography.
6. Grimes, William, b. 1784—Family.   7. King George County (Va.)—Biography.
8. New Haven (Conn.)—Biography.   9. Slaves' writings, American.
I. Andrews, William L., 1946–   II. Mason, Regina E.
III. Title.
E444.G85A3 2008
306.3'62092—dc22   2007050092

Printed in the United States of America
on acid-free paper

In memory of
Aunt Katherine Victoria Strothers Webb, for sowing the seeds of the ancestors
And to Brandon, Noelle, and Shelly

—REM

Preface

This edition of the *Life of William Grimes, the Runaway Slave, Written by Himself* had its genesis in a series of letters and emails between Regina Mason, who initiated the exchange, and Bill Andrews, who knew nothing about Regina or the research that she had been pursuing for years on William Grimes. In the fall of 1998, Regina, a native Californian, decided to send Bill, a professor at the University of North Carolina at Chapel Hill, whom she knew only by reputation, samplings from her research. What she had learned through years of painstaking investigation was that William Grimes (1784–1865) was her great-great-great-grandfather. In addition to her remarkable ancestry, Regina had also recovered the story of how her family had grown from its Connecticut roots to its California branches.

Regina knew that Bill was one of the few scholars who had studied and written about Grimes's autobiography. In his 1986 book *To Tell a Free Story,* Bill had pronounced Grimes the author of the first fugitive slave narrative in American letters. Regina wanted Bill to know about her work because she felt if there was one academic that would be receptive to her research on William Grimes it would be Bill. Neither scholar, historian, nor college graduate, Regina was seeking guidance. She felt she needed the backing of a scholar to help authenticate the volume of research she had compiled on Grimes and his family. Regina also felt strongly that William Grimes's voice needed to be heard once again. Since no other academic had taken much interest in her work, Regina didn't know if Bill would either. But she decided to risk sending him a few pages from an unpublished document she had written outlining the body of her research.

Bill responded to what Regina sent him with gratitude and enthusiasm. "I was impressed by how much you've found and where you've gone to reconstruct the genealogy of your family and of Mr. Grimes," he wrote. "You asked for my criticism and guidance, but I fear I don't have much of either to offer you. I can't criticize what seems to me to be thorough and illuminating.... You have quite a story to tell in weaving all these threads together into a coherent narrative.... The wealth of information you have uncovered ought to be preserved and published in some fashion."

In August of 1999, Regina informed Bill in an email that further work on her genealogical project had revealed that "Grimes's youngest daughter (my great-great-grandmother) was a pioneer of the West, who was very much respected in San Francisco as a dramatic performer and who, for a number of years, had a 'Colored Dramatic Troupe' that performed in some of San Francisco's early opera houses." Regina also noted that the Bay Area had begun to show an interest in her work. In October of 1998, "KQED television of San Francisco aired a 4-part segment on my research," she noted, "which was the local follow-up to the acclaimed *Africans in America* documentary" that had aired nationally on PBS in the fall of 1998.

Regina was curious about a Web site, North American Slave Narratives, that Bill had recently launched with the UNC Library. The site aimed to create for the first time a complete digital library of all the autobiographies composed by those who had endured enslavement in the North America. When, Regina wondered, would the *Life of William Grimes* appear on the site? Bill replied that he hadn't yet been able to obtain a copy of the *Life* that was suitable for scanning and digitizing. In May of 2000, Regina put him in touch with the curator of the Whitney Library at the New Haven Colony Historical Society. Just as Regina promised, the society willingly loaned a copy of the 1855 edition of the *Life* to UNC so that this narrative could become available to Internet readers around the world. By the summer of 2001, through Regina's good offices, North American Slave Narratives featured the full texts of both the 1825 and the 1855 versions of Grimes's pioneering narrative.

After a three-year hiatus, Regina emailed Bill again in the fall of 2004, asking if he would review a long personal essay she was on the verge of completing, an account of her research on Grimes and his descendants in California, Connecticut, and Virginia. This gripping essay interwove fragments of family lore; conversations with a great-aunt about an elusive family Bible; an account of a murder in an eighteenth-century Virginia newspaper; a visit to a seventeenth-century plantation; citations from Connecticut property, census, and marriage records; a search for a burial site in a cemetery across the street from Yale University—all punctuating a chronicle of the life of William Grimes and the family he began with his wife, Clarissa Caesar, in 1819. After reading this essay, Bill realized that Regina was not simply an indefatigable and relentless researcher. She also had constructed a fascinating story about how and why she had undertaken her research, to complement all she knew about the life of William Grimes and the African American family that had descended from him.

After Bill praised her essay, Regina announced yet another discovery of hers: "I have in my possession copies of preserved letters negotiating Grimes's freedom. The last letter dated April 21, 1824, is from master Welman agreeing to free Grimes for about $500. The first letter is dated August 1823." These new documents, along with everything else she had done to recover William Grimes from undeserved obscurity, led Bill to broach the idea of their collaborating on a new edition of William Grimes's *Life* that would showcase the wealth of Regina's research on and knowledge of her singular ancestor. When Regina agreed to coedit the book with him, the process of preparing the *Life* for publication began early in 2005.

The backbone of this edition of Grimes's 1855 *Life* is the annotations that authenticate much of what Grimes wrote about his career in slavery and freedom as he recalled it in the pages of his autobiography, which he first published in 1825 and, thirty years later, reprinted with an update. Most of the notes to the text are founded on Regina's

exhaustive individual research. We regret that this reader's edition of
Grimes's life isn't the place to record all available details pertaining to,
for instance, the relationship of Benjamin Grymes, William's father,
to George Washington or the identities of Connecticut notables and
Savannah slaveholders whom Grimes dealt with (whether he wanted
to or not). For the sake of conciseness, the annotations to this text focus
on what the editors believe to be the most important facts and biblio-
graphical data that confirm or illuminate the claims Grimes makes in
his *Life*.

One of the many striking features of the *Life of William Grimes* is that
its author created this pioneering autobiography on his own, without asking anyone, white or black, to help him with the writing. Nor
did Grimes solicit recommendation letters or other authenticating
documents from whites in an attempt to validate his own reliability
and truthfulness. Readers of fugitive slave narratives know that even
the most famous texts in this tradition, such as those by Frederick
Douglass and Harriet Jacobs, contain prefaces or appended statements
from white supporters and sponsors designed to convince white readers that the African American author's account of slavery is worthy of
trust. Grimes, however, launched the fugitive slave narrative tradition
in the United States quite independent, as far as we can tell, of white
support, either editorial, moral, or financial. The significance of this
go-it-alone attitude is discussed at greater length in the introduction
to this book.

As Grimes's twenty-first century editors, Regina and Bill provide authenticating and explanatory annotations to Grimes's story
because we wish to pay tribute to the author's memory and veracity.
We also believe that some truths, such as the identity of his father,
which even Grimes would not unveil despite his generally no-holds-
barred account of his life, ought to be acknowledged today. We hope
that our annotations will confirm that, though in some ways inex-
perienced as a writer, Grimes was both competent and reliable as a
personal historian. Because his autobiography records relatively few
dates, our edition of the *Life* provides a chronology of the author's
life and times that pegs his comings and goings to major events in
the history of the United States during the turbulent era in which
William Grimes lived.

The essay that introduces the *Life* is designed to provide an analysis of the originality of Grimes's autobiography when placed in its proper historical context. A handful of narratives by men who had been enslaved in North America preceded Grimes's narrative, but no African American before Grimes had authored an account of his enslavement in the American South, flight from bondage, and experience in the so-called free states of the North. No African American before Grimes had written so personally and with such emotional honesty about the violent world of slavery. No fugitive slave before or after him would speak with such candor about the struggles he had endured to preserve his quasi-freedom in a white supremacist North.

William Grimes's contribution to the literature of American slavery has been only slightly recognized up to now. It is our hope that the introduction to this edition will help readers of today see why Grimes's autobiography was truly a turning point in the history of the African American slave narrative. The introductory essay is also designed to introduce readers to Grimes himself, a fascinating and complex man whose personality suffuses his autobiography, making it a lively and provocative self-portrait unlike any published in the African American slave narrative tradition.

The edition of the *Life* reprinted in this volume is the second of Grimes's two autobiographies published by the author in New Haven, Connecticut, in 1855. The 1855 edition incorporates the original 1825 edition of the *Life* but adds a short conclusion that highlights miscellaneous instances drawn from the intervening three decades and finishes on a relatively placid note, markedly different in tone from the bitter ending of the 1825 edition. Although the groundbreaking 1825 edition constitutes Grimes's lasting contribution to the fugitive slave narrative, since the 1855 edition incorporates the entirety of the earlier edition along with an update that sheds some light on Grimes's fate since 1825, the editors believe the last edition of the *Life* is the most informative one for twenty-first century readers.

This annotated edition preserves every word of the 1855 text. To enhance its readability, however, we have sometimes broken the narrative into shorter paragraphs whenever the prose in the original edition extends for pages and pages without a paragraph break. If Grimes had availed himself of an editor in either 1825 or 1855, he might have punctuated, as well as paragraphed, his narrative in ways that would have conformed more closely to the composition and publishing practices of his day. Nevertheless, our practice has been to alter Grimes's spelling or punctuation only to correct silently obvious printer's errors. Except for fashioning several shorter paragraphs from a prolix one and inserting in square brackets—[ ]—a name or word when pronoun antecedents aren't clear, we have preserved Grimes's words, punctuation, and capitalization exactly as they appear in the 1855 *Life*.

Regina's afterword reflects on her personal research odyssey and the circumstances that led her to pursue the once shadowy Grimes of family lore. In addition to taking readers through the highs and lows of her search for Grimes, her essay also provides a glimpse of the world into which she, as a child, was thrust as the Civil Rights movement gave rise to the Black Power era in her native Oakland neighborhood. Sparked by a fifth-grade class assignment on origins, her story is about a young girl's struggle for identity, her place in the world, and her roots. For Regina, genealogy makes history truer and more complete by revealing the lives of seemingly ordinary citizens who, in their own circumstances and surroundings, have contributed richly to the fabric of their communities and ultimately this country. Her hope is that her afterword will inspire the general public and especially students to find the hidden treasures in their own family trees and then write about them.

The introduction and afterword to this edition serve as bookends for the central text in this book, the *Life of William Grimes, the Runaway Slave, Written by Himself*. This framing of Grimes's story by a biracial editorial partnership, each of whom has made a distinctive but complementary contribution to this collaboration, seems to us historically meaningful. Perhaps William Grimes chose to write and publish his autobiography on his own because he was too proud to ask anyone to help him or because he was suspicious of possible interference or exploitation if he solicited a white person's aid. In any case, scholarship on the African American slave narrative has raised unsettling questions about the power relationship among white editors, sponsors, and publishers when they engaged a fugitive slave, whether literate or not, in an autobiographical enterprise.

Looking back on this history, we view our editing of Grimes's *Life* as both a productive equal partnership and a satisfying revisionary alternative to the power imbalances based on race that governed the publication of so many slave narratives in the nineteenth century. We are glad to have found common ground and common purpose in our own editorial work. Each one of us has learned from the other. The outcome—this edition—represents the best that our independent research and judgment could have brought to this unprecedented collaboration and to the singular autobiography that gave us the rare opportunity to work together.

William L. Andrews
Regina E. Mason

Acknowledgments

I, Regina Mason, owe a debt of gratitude to many. In the early years, when Grimes was still a conjecture of family lore, staff from the El Cerrito Library, the Richmond Public Library, and the Oakland Public Library introduced me to a man named William Grimes. At the same time that I conducted a historical search for Grimes, staff from several genealogical institutions and local historical societies gave freely of their knowledge in ways that revealed the branches in my family tree: the Oakland Regional Family History Center, the California State Library-Sutro, the San Francisco History Center, as well as the San Francisco African-American Historical and Cultural Society. Other Bay Area repositories that aided my quest were the National Archives Pacific Sierra Region in San Bruno as well as the National Archives in Washington, DC and the Cecil H. Green Library at Stanford University. The specific works of Rudolph Lapp and John Templeton whose research on black San Francisco made plain to me the important early contributions of blacks in the San Francisco Bay Area and throughout California.

On the East Coast the following people, whose names are indelibly etched in my mind, in association with their institutions, made considerable contributions to this project. Katherine Keene Fields, Director of the Litchfield Historical Society, generously gave copies of whatever documents the society owned on Grimes. Dr. Lynne Templeton Brickley Project Historian with the Litchfield Historical Society not only shared with me her study on Grimes in Litchfield, but also offered her transcriptions of preserved letters negotiating his freedom. Sincere thanks goes to James Campbell, Librarian and Curator of Manuscripts, at the Whitney Library in New Haven, who gave tirelessly to my constant barrage of questions—even special requests—pertaining to Grimes in New Haven. Actor Guy Peartree is also deserving of my thanks for his emotionally moving interpretation of *Old Grimes*, as is Barbara W. Winters of the Dixwell Avenue Congregational United Church of Christ who not only steered me to the Amos Beman Scrapbooks at Yale, but also graciously dug up and copied old records pertaining to the old Temple Street Church where early family appears in church records.

Peter Hinks gave insight into the Lanson brothers of black New Haven; Randall Burkett on the Reverend Harry Croswell. Wendy W. Schnur, Reference Manager at the G. W. Blunt White Library, Mystic, Connecticut, tracked the comings and goings of the *Casket*; Bill Cameron of the Grove Street Cemetery gave assistance in uncovering those interred in the Grimes Family Plot; Richard Seldon actually found the plot and generated media publicity while in New Haven. Staff from the Connecticut State Library, the Sterling Memorial Library, and the Beinecke Rare Book Library also deserve my thanks, as does Elizabeth C. Bouvier, Head of Archives, Supreme Judicial Court of Massachusetts.

In the Southeast, Jon Yagla, present owner of Eagle's Nest, not only shared information about his historical property; he and his wife graciously opened their home to my mother and me. Linda Adair, formerly of the Lewis Egerton Smoot Library in King George, Virginia, generously shared resources on the history of Eagle's Nest. Staff at the Virginia Historical Society forwarded rare newspapers of the murder that took place on the grounds of Eagle's Nest. The Library of Virginia and the Earl Gregg Swem Library in Williamsburg produced documents pertaining to the Fitzhugh and Grymes families as did George Washington's Mount Vernon Estate and Gardens. Several staff members at the Georgia Historical Society tracked some of the owners of William Grimes in Savannah; John A. W. Wolhaupter corresponded with me about his ancestor Philip David Woolhopter, to whom William Grimes was hired out. Tricia Petitt provided genealogies on the Stuart and Thornton families of Virginia; and Bob Thornton, distant cousin of Col. William Thornton, sent me a massive document on the research he had done on the Thornton's still-standing Montpelier Estate. Sharon DeBartolo Carmack donated many hours in search of William Grimes's elusive mother, whom I may never know by name.

An extra special thank-you goes to Elissa Moncheian at the University of California at Berkeley, Interlibrary Borrowing Service, in Doe Library, who went the extra mile in accessing materials from all over the United States pertaining to the life of William Grimes; staff from the Bancroft Library, also at Berkeley, exposed me to the work of Delilah Beasley and the collection of Jeremiah B. Sanderson, in which I found references to my foremother, Clarissa Grimes Williams, the remarkable tragedienne. I must also acknowledge the richly important work of the indefatigable bibliophile, the late James de Abajain.

Heartfelt thanks go to the following professionals who offered their unique expertise, advice, and encouragement along the way: Charles L. Blockson, the late Kennell Jackson, Deanne Hamilton, Avon Kirkland, Barbara Gates, and Neil Henry. Finally, it is with deep admiration and gratitude that I thank Bill Andrews for believing in my work, for taking me under his wing, and for mentoring me every step of the way through this enormous project.

Bill and I offer sincerest thanks to Anne Bruder, who checked annotations and provided a great deal of thoughtful research assistance and fact-checking for this edition. Both Bill and I appreciate the thorough work of our editors at Oxford University Press in New York.

To my ardent well-wishers in the Office of the Registrar at Berkeley, whose good cheer and encouragement propelled me to the finish line when the end seemed nowhere in sight, I offer deep appreciation.

My thanks and appreciation also go to my family, my most devoted supporters, who delighted in each and every gain to reclaim our heritage. Those most generous in time and deeds were Alex Turner, Marianne Williams, Margurite Fuller, Suzie D'Aria, Marilouse Allen, Jean Gilliam, the late Shirley DeCou, and the late Virginia Moore.

To my dear mother, Janet Turner, my fellow researcher who was there with me on many local and distant venues in the name of roots,

I offer a multitude of love and appreciation. I also thank my first research partner, my sister, Sheryl Cabrera, with whom I did the victory dance when we found our grandmother as a child in the 1900 Federal Census in California. Aside from having a personal interest in our history, over the years my brother, Rob Brown, gave freely of his craft and his employer, the Oakland Museum of California. My thanks also go to my brother-in-law Rich Cabrera, who successfully navigated us through unfamiliar East Coast territory, and to my sister-in-law, Jill Brown, for her constant encouragement.

To my late father, Robert E. Brown, my guardian angel, I know you've been with me from the start. To my nephew Kyle, my nieces Monica and Mia, and to my cherished daughters, Noelle and Michelle, may the legacy of William Grimes inspire each one of you to strive higher and to make a difference in our communities. Last, but not least by any measure, I'd like to thank my husband, Brandon. I could not have traversed this long, ever-winding, seemingly endless road of highs and lows without you.

Contents

Illustrations

Life of William Grimes,
the Runaway Slave

Introduction

William L. Andrews

William Grimes (1784–1865) authored the first fugitive slave narrative in American history in 1825, when he was slightly over forty years of age. The longest African American autobiography published up to that time,[1] the *Life of William Grimes, the Runaway Slave, Written by Himself* was motivated not so much by a reformist impulse as by personal financial need. Grimes and his family had been rendered homeless and nearly penniless in April of 1824 because of his forced decision to pay $500 for his self-purchase to his menacing Savannah, Georgia, master, from whom Grimes had escaped nine years earlier. Having been enslaved for a little more than thirty years, Grimes recounted a personal history of almost unrelieved anguish, both physical and psychological. "I endeavour," he asserted in his *Life* "to give my readers but a faint representation of the hard treatment, ill usage and horrid abuse the poor slave experiences while groaning under the yoke of bondage; that yoke which is not easy, nor the burden light; but being placed in that situation, to repine is useless, we must submit to our fate and bear up as well as we can under the cruel treatment of our despotic tyrants." No African American autobiography before Grimes's details so candidly or so relentlessly the abuse that its author suffered before escaping to freedom. Few who followed Grimes in the fugitive slave narrative tradition acknowledged as frankly as he the galling irony that was supposed freedom in the North—"this hard cold country," he called it—a place Grimes refused, at the end of his narrative, to recommend as a refuge to his fellow slaves in the South. For better and for worse, Grimes entered African American literature untutored, unsponsored, and unedited, determined to speak his mind about all he had been through: "My readers may put their own constructions and draw inferences, I can barely state that I tell the truth."

Grimes told the truth about his enslavement in Virginia and Georgia, about his struggles to establish himself in the New England, and, most of all, about himself. Although his autobiography is not notably introspective, it must have been a revelation to those northern whites who discovered the *Life* in 1825. We have no record of any reviews of the 1825 edition of Grimes's autobiography, nor do we know why Grimes chose to have it printed in New York City rather than in the thriving northwestern Connecticut town of Litchfield, where he resided when the *Life* appeared. Thirty years later, when he reprinted the *Life* with a short conclusion that provides various anecdotes about his exploits since his initial foray into print, Grimes observed that of the "large edition" he had printed in 1825, only a few copies were still available. Thus, the author proudly announced in 1855, he presented "this second edition of the Life of one who has often been called one of the most remarkable personages of modern times" to "many distinguished men of New Haven" as well as to the general public because "I believe almost everybody will purchase a copy of my Life." Since little scholarship has been done on Grimes up to now, we have no reliable information about who or how many read the first or.second edition of his autobiography, nor do we know how either narrative was received.[2]

Despite the seventy-one-year-old Grimes's inflated claim to have been "one of the most remarkable personages of modern times," he probably *had* earned for himself by 1855 an uncommon local reputation. A decade later, in his August 21, 1865, obituary, the New Haven *Daily Palladium* stated of Grimes: "All New Haven knew him, he was always on the corners of the streets, basket in hand. He was an aged gentleman" who "sold lottery tickets and was versed in theological lore....Forty years ago he was the head of a prosperous barber shop opposite the colleges. All Yale patronized him and thousands of Yale graduates knew him."[3] However, what the *Daily Palladium* also recalled about Grimes's life was the fact that after "his master came from the south to claim him as his property, Old Grimes heard and was at once a fugitive, and his barbershop trade a ruin. He returned at last but was never after his former self." The once thriving tradesman gradually "settled down into a quiet daily circuit of the thoroughfares of the city in quest of cold bits and happiness, on communion Sundays visiting the churches where the best wine was to be procured, and partaking of the Sacrament."

The eighty-one-year-old who emerges from this obituary may help us understand better the posture Grimes took before his 1855 reader. The *Daily Palladium* speaks fondly of Grimes: "He is dead that good old soul." But the comments about the old man's hand-to-mouth street-corner existence and regular visits to multiple churches for communion wine suggest an infirmity and dependency markedly at variance with the defiantly confrontational figure we meet in 1825. The conclusion to the 1855 *Life* signals changes in outlook and disposition that Grimes had undergone in the decades following the publication of his first autobiography. By 1855, the elderly Grimes professed a philosophical attitude toward his past troubles considerably mellower than anything the smoldering, resentful autobiographer of 1825 could have mustered. The 1855 conclusion blandly observes that "all the wrongs which I have met with in my eventful life have no doubt been ordered wisely." The author even claims to "have forgiven all."

How Grimes attained this perspective on the past by 1855 is unclear. The writer for the *Daily Palladium* implies that the financial and psychological costs of preserving his freedom—he "was never after his former self"—were more damaging to the former slave than even Grimes himself would have acknowledged. If so, is the conclusion of 1855 indicative of this imputed process of decline, or are the calm and acceptance of the conclusion a credit to its author's patience, faith, and fortitude? However we might answer this question, we must keep in mind that the 1855 *Life* disavows nothing asserted in 1825. Indeed, the 1855 *Life* fully reprints the 1825 first edition without repudiating a word. Thus we have no reason to believe that past wrongs, particularly those Grimes experienced in slavery, no longer mattered to him by the time he reached his

seventies. Also noteworthy is the fact that, although proclaiming forgiveness, the 1855 conclusion also asserts that the author hasn't forgotten "those persons who have oppressed poor Grimes." They, he adds,
"should recollect that although his skin is a little darker than theirs,
he yet has the feelings of a man, and knows when he is abused." This
reinvoking of his abused manhood reminds the reader that the angry
author of 1825 had not been wholly mollified three decades later.

By reprinting the complete 1855 edition of the *Life of William Grimes,
the Runaway Slave*, the editors wish to preserve the entire autobiographical record of this extraordinary man's struggle for freedom, justice, and
opportunity in the South and the North during the first half-century
of American nationhood. We remain convinced that the genius of
Grimes's pioneering contribution to the fugitive slave narrative tradition lies in the story he first told in 1825.

A chronic sense of unassuaged injury seems to have been the principal motivation that drove Grimes to undertake an autobiography. He
needed money. Hence his direct appeal to the reader's "charity" toward
a slave who, after enduring thirty years of "suffering" in bondage, had
finally "tasted the sweets of liberty" only to be stripped of "house,
home, and livelihood" by an avaricious former master. But the autobiographer's manner was more importunate than supplicant: "To him
who has feeling, the condition of a slave, under any possible circumstances, is painful and unfortunate, and will excite the sympathy of all
who have any." This challenge to the reader to prove he could sympathize with a slave indicates that Grimes was by no means sure that his
reader could or would provide the sympathy or support that Grimes
believed he deserved.

Grimes's suspicions were not unwarranted. Although black people
were more numerous in Connecticut than in the rest of New England
combined, whites had done little, aside from the passage of a gradual
emancipation act in 1784, to treat their African American neighbors
with respect.[4] Even the 1784 emancipation statute was "framed by a
web of restrictions and regulations that encoded a permanent status of
legal difference for 'Indians,' 'Molattos,' and 'Negroes.'" The statute, as
one scholar notes, was designed to ensure that the rights, security, and
welfare of Connecticut whites would remain "entitlements...from
which slaves were and would remain excluded, *regardless of their postslavery*

status" (emphasis added).[5] In 1818, Connecticut restricted the right to vote to white males, ahead of southern states such as Alabama (1819), Tennessee (1834), North Carolina (1835), Arkansas (1836), Florida (1845), and Texas (1845).[6] Connecticut's indifference, and often outright hostility, to free people of color during the time of William Grimes explains why the 1825 *Life* contains no sign of its author's counting on antislavery sentiment to arouse the sympathy and support he sought.[7] The end of the 1855 edition may display a contented Grimes happily basking in "the kind regards of the good people of New Haven." But more memorable and important is the edgy, mistrustful Grimes of 1825, admittedly "embittered" by what he had been through, with no one to recommend or defend him, yet almost demanding a full hearing and fair treatment nonetheless.

This was not the tone or the rhetorical posture deployed by the relatively few African Americans who composed their autobiographies before Grimes. The large majority of African American personal narratives that antedate Grimes's narrative were attributed to condemned, usually enslaved criminals whose "dying confessions" recounted, almost ritually, the dire consequences they faced after having rejected the white authority figures in their lives and plunging into the chaos of their own selfish appetites. The fact that many of these black murderers and rapists had run away from slavery before undertaking their violent, self-destructive careers did nothing to encourage the kind of sympathy for a fugitive slave that Grimes hoped to engender.[8] The implicit ethical argument of Grimes's autobiography suggests that a slave is justified in resisting and fleeing a brutalizing bondage rather than acquiescing to inevitable exploitation and demoralization. But black criminal confessions of the late eighteenth and early nineteenth centuries almost never ask why a slave ran away, much less what may have driven him to become a criminal. Instead, these confession narratives argue implicitly that the slave is at home in bondage and safest when monitored by the providential authority of master, the white social order, and God's will. Even when a sympathetic black interviewer presided over the scene of autobiographical confession, the all-too-ready conclusion to be drawn was that the condemned black man's guilt could be traced to his having been "a slave of Sin."[9] In most early African American autobiographies, the slavery of sin received much more condemnation than the sin of slavery.

Only a handful of slave narratives before Grimes's protest the widespread presumption of white North America that slavery was a divinely appointed means of civilizing and Christianizing people of African descent. In *The Blind African Slave, or Memoirs of Boyrereau Brinch, Nicknamed Jeffrey Brace* (1810), a collaborative narrative produced by the African-born Brace and a white Vermont lawyer, Benjamin Prentiss (who identifies himself as "the author" of the text),[10] slavery in Barbados, where Brace first arrived after his experience of the Middle Passage, and in Connecticut, where Brace endured many cruelties from a succession of masters between 1763 and 1777, is pictured as brutal and barbaric. In the penultimate paragraph of *The Blind African Slave*, the narrator states his antislavery position unequivocally: "I have concluded it my duty to myself, to all Africans who can read, to the Church, in short to all mankind, to thus publish these my memoirs, that all may see how poor Africans have been and perhaps now are abused by a christian and enlightened people. Being old and blind, almost destitute of property, it may bring me something to make me comfortable in my declining days, but above all, it is my anxious wish that this simple narrative may be the means of opening the hearts of those who hold slaves and move them to consent to give them that freedom which they themselves enjoy, and which all mankind have an equal right to possess."[11] Deploring the inhumanity of slavery, Brace's plea articulates the "moral suasionist" stance assumed by many white early American antislavery adherents. A devout Christian, Brace entrusts the abolition of slavery to a process of "opening hearts," which will move slaveholders to "consent" voluntarily to the manumission of their human property.[12] Unlike that of Grimes, Brace's faith was strong enough to enable him to bear his sufferings until he could extricate himself from slavery by legal means. In 1777, Brace enlisted in the Continental Army and, at war's end, mustered out, having secured his freedom by virtue of his five years of service as a soldier in the American Revolution.

In the same year that saw *The Blind African Slave* published in Vermont, another black evangelical published his autobiography, *A Brief Account of the Life, Experience, Travels, and Gospel Labours of George White, an African; Written by Himself, and Revised by a Friend*, in New York. White's narrative deals almost entirely with his conversion, his evolving sense of spiritual calling to the ministry, and the arduous process by which he eventually received ordination as a full-fledged preacher in the predominantly white Methodist Church. White acknowledges, albeit briefly, that he spent his first twenty-six years enslaved in Virginia before being manumitted through the will of his dying master. Before moving on to his spiritual pilgrimage, White pauses long enough to censure slavery in the abstract: "Perhaps nothing can be more conducive to vice and immorality, than a state of abject slavery, like that practised by the Virginia planters upon the degraded Africans."[13] Nevertheless, what little White says about the miserable condition of "the degraded Africans" tends toward blaming the victim: "For being deprived by their inhuman masters and overseers, of almost every privilege and enjoyment, in their absence, without much restraint or reserve, [the slaves] fall into those practices, which are contrary to the well-being of society, and repugnant to the will of God, whenever opportunity offers."[14] White insists that the trend of his own upward career, despite "adversity, pain, and sickness"—not to mention persistent (though unacknowledged) racial discrimination at the hands of established ministers—proves that all misfortunes are but tests of the spirit, since "whom the Lord loveth he chasteneth."[15]

One reason that William Grimes's 1825 intervention into black American autobiography is so remarkable is his singular refusal to attribute his adversity and pain in both slavery and freedom to a divine design to reinforce his faith. In this regard Grimes diverges significantly from White's autobiography and from the way Solomon Bayley chose to interpret his abortive attempt to escape his enslavement in his *Narrative of Some Remarkable Incidents, in the Life of Solomon Bayley, Formerly a Slave, in the State of Delaware, North America: Written by Himself* (1825). Bayley follows the conventions of the early African American slave narrative in portraying his 1799 trek from Richmond, Virginia, to Camden, Delaware, primarily as a spiritual quest rather than as a desperate bid for individual freedom. Before recounting his harrowing journey, Bayley confesses his guilt for "having sinned against God; whom if I had been careful to obey in all things, he would have spared me all my troubles."[16] Thus through the narration of his actual escape, Bayley identifies himself as a "sinner," not a slave, a "stranger in distress," not a fugitive hiding out from slave-holding authorities. Maybe Bayley thought that white readers would be more favorably disposed toward him if he played down his black fugitive identity in favor of a more familiar and popularly sanctioned self-image as a Christian wayfarer in a world of trials. Nevertheless, by subsuming his black individuality, with all its inherent social and political significance as a commentary on the injustice of slavery,[17] under a generic identity—a Christian seeking God's merciful redemption—Bayley invites his reader to regard his personal story as simply a metaphor of Everyman's spiritual struggles. As long as African American autobiography allowed slavery to be represented as a spiritual trial to be welcomed rather than as a sociopolitical injustice to be resisted, white readers would learn little about the real-world evils of slavery or why the institution had to be repudiated.

The slave narrator who anticipates Grimes most strikingly was Venture Smith, whose *A Narrative of the Life and Adventures of Venture, a Native of Africa* (1798) recounts a rough-and-tumble existence as a slave and freedman in Connecticut that would surely have resonated with William Grimes. Smith's recollections of his enslavement depict the same recalcitrance and, when pushed to the limit, physical resistance to slave-holding violence that we find in Grimes's account of his own bondage. Among all the early African American autobiographers, Smith has the least to say about the spiritual or religious side of his life. He never mentions Christ or Christianity, except on one occasion to denounce the hypocrisy of the "christian" land of Connecticut when compared to his native Africa.[18] Smith's story concentrates on his hard-nosed pursuit of the material goods of this world, which he accumulated with a degree of success that a man on the make like Grimes would surely have admired, especially given the latter's firsthand knowledge of white bigotry in Connecticut.

Smith's *Narrative* details the harshness of slavery in New England, which he bore until the age of thirty-six, when he purchased his freedom through legal means. Thereafter he has little to say about slavery and nothing directly critical of it as an institution. He acknowledges, in fact, that during several short instances he himself had become a slave owner, although he suggests that he did so only to help the men he purchased.[19] In the concluding paragraph of his narrative, Smith avows, "My freedom is a privilege which nothing else can equal." But the most explicit statements about the injustice of slavery in Smith's *Narrative* come from the unnamed, presumably white, amanuensis of the *Narrative*.

"The subject of the following pages," the preface to the *Narrative* states, "had he received only a common education, might have been a man of high respectability and usefulness; and had his education been suited to his genius, he might have been an ornament and an honor to human nature. It may perhaps, not be unpleasing to see the efforts of a great mind wholly uncultivated, enfeebled and depressed by slavery, and struggling under every disadvantage."[20] That Smith's amanuensis, ostensibly his supporter, could think of no other way to express his opposition to slavery than to lament the respectable person Smith "might have been" if only he hadn't been "enfeebled" by slavery is troubling. Smith's inspiring accomplishments in freedom, rather than what his enslavement had done to "depress" him, might have been the argument of someone more committed to paying tribute to the achievements of an individual black man against considerable odds. Smith's editor, however, seems to have believed that for an antislavery argument to be most compelling, it needed to stress how the slave's or former slave's victimization by slavery had made him a pitiable, though instructive, object to other whites.

If William Grimes came across a copy of Smith's *Narrative* during Grimes's early years in Connecticut, the ambivalence of the unnamed white editor toward the former slave, predicated on a premise that to have been enslaved was to be permanently disqualified from "high respectability and usefulness," may have led to Grimes's decision to write and publish his autobiography himself. Almost all nineteenth-century slave narratives that are celebrated today—including those by Moses Roper, Frederick Douglass, William Wells Brown, Henry Bibb, Sojourner Truth, and Harriet Jacobs—were introduced, edited, published, or otherwise "authenticated" by white sponsors and supporters solicited to bolster the credibility and spread the publicity of the narratives they endorsed.[21] In stark contrast, the 1825 *Life of William Grimes* is conspicuous for the absence of white participation in the production or publication of the text itself. Unlike not only his predecessors but also his most famous mid-nineteenth-century successors in the slave narrative tradition, Grimes was plainly determined to represent himself on his own before the bar of public opinion both as former slave deserving freedom and as black autobiographer bent on getting a white hearing.

We can do little more than speculate on why Grimes's autobiography was among the first in African American literary history to feature the arresting, politically charged subtitle, *Written by Himself*.[22] The subtitle spoke proudly, even audaciously, of any black man's authorial agency at a time when many whites, even in the North, regarded literacy as solely their racial prerogative. The same subtitle, of course, could denote literary isolation as well as independence. Did Grimes write his autobiography by himself because he did not hope to secure white assistance or support for the undertaking? Or did he resolve from the outset to set a black literary precedent in American autobiography? We do not know. Twenty years later, Frederick Douglass and other fugitive slave autobiographers not only claimed the *Written by Himself* subtitle but also structured their memoirs around the slave's ceaseless quest for proscribed literacy and knowledge. The *Life of William Grimes*, by contrast, says nothing about how the author learned to read or write, whether in slavery or freedom. "I have learned to read and write pretty well," Grimes remarks in 1825, adding, with his usual aplomb, "if I had an opportunity I could learn very fast."[23] Thirty years later, Grimes had nothing more to say about the matter.

Grimes's record of self-reliance in slavery and freedom strongly suggests that once he had conceived of his ambitious autobiographical project, his contentious ego, as well as the novelty of the project itself, would likely have kept it in his hands alone. He drily acknowledges that even as a slave, he was "perhaps, difficult to *govern in the way in which it was attempted.*" His often frustrating experience in the courts of Connecticut—recalling one trial, Grimes claims that "if I had plead my own case, I could have done better than any lawyer"—may have had something to do with his extraordinary literary self-determination. Moreover, Grimes's long-standing sense of aggrievement—"It has been my fortune most always to be suspected by the good, and to be cheated and abused by the vicious"—probably fueled his desire, if not his need, to tell his story fully and freely in his own way. It is a mark of the premium he placed on candor that at the end of the 1825 edition of his *Life*, he admits, "I cannot speak as I feel on some subjects." But this seems to be an indication of self-censorship, not a yielding to another's agenda. Whatever the source or motive, whether by necessity or by choice, Grimes's go-it-alone strategy made his the originating, unforgettable voice of the first fugitive slave in African American letters.

An altogether singular, colloquial, and candid voice it is, eloquent and incisive at times, abrasive and self-serving at other times. Grimes begins his account in a fashion that would become formulaic in the slave narrative by the 1850s. He writes: "I was born in the year 1784, in J—, County of King George, Virginia, in a land boasting its freedom, and under a government whose motto is Liberty and Equality. I was yet born a slave." Invoking from the outset the fundamental irony of chattel slavery in a supposedly free country (the United States was in its first year of national existence when Grimes was born) helped Grimes lay the groundwork for the indignation that suffuses so much of his autobiography. The same irony, as though heightened, not tempered, by forty years of slavery and freedom, erupts in the final two sentences of the 1825 *Life*. Anticipating his death, Grimes proffers a sardonically grisly bequest: "If it were not for the stripes on my back which were made when I was a slave, I would in my will leave my skin as a legacy to the government, desiring that it might be taken off and made into parchment, and then bind the constitution of glorious, happy and *free* America. Let the skin of an American slave bind the charter of American liberty!"

The intervening sixty-seven pages of the 1825 *Life* read less like a review of Grimes's past than like the record of his psyche in the act of reviving, reliving, and sometimes revenging himself on the past. Opening Grimes's book almost anywhere feels like reopening the man's wounds of mind and body. No slave narrator in America before Grimes made such painful self-revelation a hallmark of his personal address.

The focus of Grimes's attention in recounting his experience of enslavement is on excruciating personal memories, not the experience of enslavement as his peers underwent it. In Grimes's telling, the one constant in his life from boyhood to adulthood in slavery was unmerited cruelty and violence at the hands of slaveholders, overseers, and black slave drivers. "The disposition to tyrannize over those under us is universal; and there is no one who will not occasionally do it," Grimes grants in one of the moments when he stops to ponder the reason for the pervasive violence of slavery. For the most part, however, he writes more like a prosecutor than an analyst. He marshals evidence from scene after bloody scene in which he was "horsed up," knocked down, beaten with fists, whipped with hickory sticks, clubbed into submission, and flogged until unconscious. He recalls beatings meted out to slave women as well as to men. He shocks his reader with this terse image of the back of a fellow flogging victim: "I could compare it to nothing but a field lately ploughed."

Why does Grimes log so many of these atrocities as he narrates his own years of enslavement? The fact that he repeatedly insists on his own innocence in the face of many of these beatings suggests his concern that his white New England readers might have thought him deserving of such punishment if he had not made a point of stressing otherwise. Grimes may well have felt that he had to amass overwhelming evidence of his unjust suffering in slavery in order to convince whites in Connecticut to sympathize with him, rather than dismiss him simply as a fractious runaway slave who should have, by rights, returned to his master. If the sensational quality of Grimes's stories of beatings and whippings attracted whites for less than humanitarian reasons, one can hardly doubt that Grimes was content to achieve his desired ends— a profitable sale—however oblique the means.

Grimes was among the earliest slave narrators to lament and protest his early separation from his mother because of the callousness of slaveholders. In the process he introduced into the African American slave narrative one of its most emotionally telling themes, the destructive effect of slavery on the black family: "It grieved me to see my mother's tears at our separation. I was a heart-broken child, although too young to realize the afflictions of a tender mother, who was also a slave, the hopes of freedom for her already lost; but I was compelled to go and leave her." Later slave narrators would dramatize more skillfully scenes in which families were parted at auctions and at other commercial transactions. Many of Grimes's successors were more adept at individualizing their own mothers in their stories. Nevertheless, Grimes's attachment to and pity for his lost mother are plain. The image of his motherless boyhood is designed to elicit some of the sympathy Grimes courted from his reader. But the author's conflicted feelings about the white Virginia aristocrat who was his father speak to an even deeper need for respect that impelled Grimes to resist slavery and to seek freedom and opportunity in the North.

"I had too much sense and feeling to be a slave," Grimes explains early in his autobiography, "too much of the blood of my father, whose spirit feared nothing." How much Grimes identified with his blue-blooded Virginia patrimony is a complex and intriguing question.[24] Readers of the *Life* will judge for themselves the significance of Grimes's ambivalence about his own color and his allotted place on the American color line. That the issue was central to his own sense of himself is clear from the opening sentence of his autobiography. By way of introducing himself to those who "wish to know who Grimes is," the author first announces his Litchfield residence, then his age, and then that he is "married to a black woman, and passes for a negro, although three parts white." Pointedly noting his marriage to "a black woman" may indicate that Grimes was unashamedly, even proudly, black-identified. But if in Savannah, as the *Life* informs us later, Grimes delighted in passing for a white man,[25] what is his purpose in stating from the outset that he "passes for" a Negro, "although three parts white," in Litchfield? Is Grimes dissatisfied with his "negro" designation or only with the discrimination he met probably daily in Connecticut because of it? Is he raising a challenge from the start of his story to the American racial pecking order, which relegated a man "three parts white" to Negro status? Or does Grimes's autobiography imply that passing for white in the South or Negro in the North were both racial performances that a mixed-race person would be obliged to learn for reasons ranging from spite to survival? However we might answer these questions, if Grimes did object to his racial profile, not to mention his status, in Connecticut, he was not as vocal about that as he was in protesting his treatment as a slave in the South. Nevertheless, the occasional instances of color prejudice in the North that crop up in the *Life* opened up a line of discourse to which a number of later comparatively light-skinned African Americans, including practically all the most famous fugitive slave narrators of the mid-nineteenth century, contributed, often by presenting their own near-whiteness as demonstrable refutations of the equation of "Negro" and "slave" in popular consciousness.

"My father, ——, was one of the most wealthy planters in Virginia," Grimes announces early in his autobiography. Pointing out that "in all the Slave States the children follow the condition of their mother," Grimes drives his reader to an indecorous but inescapable conclusion:

"I was in law, a bastard and a slave." The author thereby doubly alienated from social respectability, Grimes's admission of his bastardy and bondage suggests that the niceties of American filiopiety mean nothing to him. Yet he goes on writing about his father, expressing feelings more self-revealing than any that Roper, Douglass, Brown, and Bibb—all of them, like Grimes, the products of illicit sexual relationships between slaveholders and enslaved women—would later acknowledge.

Grimes's refusal actually to name his father in the *Life* may betray the son's lingering deference to his white forebear's reputation and standing. "My father, I have no doubt, would have bought and freed me," Grimes claims, "if I had not been sold and taken off while he was in jail." Yet, "I then thought and now speak on the subject [of his father] with indifference.... That he suffered his blood to run in the veins of a slave, is the only reflection I would cast upon his memory, which is just none at all in the Slave States." We may accept Grimes's claim to an indifference toward his father matching that of his father toward his mixed-race son, but such casualness does not jibe with the author's proud assertion later in the story that it was his father's fearless blood that fueled his resistance to enslavement. If Grimes felt his father's blood made him a resister of oppression, perhaps his irascibility about color discrimination in the North stemmed, at least in part, from a sense of his having not received the respect due him as a near-white man.[26]

The *Life of William Grimes, the Runaway Slave* broached many of the grim truths about slavery that later, now classic, fugitive slave narratives of the 1840s and 1850s made almost their stock in trade. Roper, Douglass, Brown, Bibb, and other well-known fugitives gave their readers a thorough accounting of the awful facts of day-to-day deprivation that was the lot of the average slave in the American South. The antislavery movement wanted slave narratives to document the inadequate and unwholesome rations, squalid and filthy living conditions, paltry bodily covering, unmet health needs, and punishing dawn-to-dusk routinized labor suffered by slaves in the South. The aim was to tear the mask off proslavery pretensions of slaveholders' paternal regard for their bondmen and women so as to construct an open-and-shut case against the institution. In 1825, Grimes was not as systematic or as comprehensive in surveying the everyday evils of slavery as later slave narrators were. Nevertheless, his descriptions of the toil and living conditions he had to endure provide readers with a gut-level sense of slavery's severity. He has an eye for the physically repellant, and therefore more memorable, detail: "The lice were so thick and large that I was obliged to spread a blanket (which I had procured myself) on the floor [of a jail he was sent to], and as they crawled upon it, take a junk or porter bottle, which I found in the jail, and roll it over the blanket repeatedly" to kill them.

Grimes's indictment of slavery places a premium on self-disclosure, as though the best way to expose the outrageousness of enslavement was to demonstrate, in his own person and behavior, the extremes to which a slave might be forced to go. Later slave narratives also spoke of what they called the slaves' "degradation," but in general terms it rarely applied to the slave narrator himself. Frederick Douglass, for instance, recalled that his master's indifference to his own hunger was one of the most insupportable features of his experience of slavery. The one-eighth bushel of cornmeal that he and each of his fellow slaves received as their weekly allowances reduced them "to the wretched necessity of living at the expense of our neighbors. This we did by begging and stealing, whichever came handy in the time of need, the one being considered as legitimate as the other."[27] Douglass knew that he didn't need to go any further than to speak of thievery as a "legitimate" response to hunger in order to score a direct hit on the perverse institution of slavery.

Twenty years earlier, Grimes had made a point of recounting the lengths to which slaves would go to appease their aching hunger. But Grimes's account is more graphic and self-revealing, even self-demeaning, than Douglass's account, and it doesn't conclude with a moral:

> Colonel Thornton was a severe master, and he made his slaves work harder than any one about there, and kept them poorer. Sometimes we had a little meat, or fish, but not often anything more than our peck of meal. We used to steal meat whenever we could get a chance; and such was my craving for it, that if the punishment had been death, I could not have resisted the temptation. How much I suffered, I will not pretend to say; but I recollect one Saturday I had been to work hard all day: in the evening, I found, back of the garden, some hog's entrails

which had been thrown out a few days before. I was so hungry
for meat, that I took these guts, washed them, and put them
into a skillet and boiled them. I then wet some corn meal in
cold water, put it in the ashes, and made a fire over it. After it
had baked, I mixed it with the guts and eat it; but before morning I was so much swollen that I liked to have died. When any
of the hogs died, we always eat them. But we did not wait for
pigs and geese to die of old age, when we could get a chance to
steal them. Steal? Yes, steal them. Why, I have been so hungry
for meat that I could have eat my mother.

Douglass's reference to the desperate survival ethic that slaves were
obliged to adopt in a state of near-starvation is brief, dispassion-
ate, and relatively cerebral. Grimes's shocking but riveting anecdote
mixes suspense, disgust, and pathos to personalize the extremity of his
own gut-wrenching need for subsistence. His supremely disturbing
admission—"I have been so hungry for meat that I could have eat my
mother"—abandons nineteenth-century sentimentality about sacrifi-
cial motherhood on the way to taking an even greater risk: invoking
white anxieties about African cannibalism in order to speak the brutal
truth about the power of slavery-induced deprivation to push anyone
to the limits of self-preservation in order to survive.

The southern plantation as rural chamber of horrors, a nightmare
world presided over by capricious, bestial whites to whom violence and
cruelty were a way of life, became a standardized image in many slave
narratives of the 1840s and 1850s. In 1825, Grimes provided the first tour
of this terrifying Hobbesian world, of which few of his northern readers
had any direct knowledge. In the South, according to Grimes, whites
and blacks coexist uneasily on a margin of extreme daily duress. Violence in word and deed can and does explode regularly, sometimes for
no apparent reason at all. Profanity—usually bowdlerized in later slave
narratives—punctuates the speech of Grimes's slaveholders, a verbal
token of their propensity to combat. Far from suffering in silence,
Grimes replies with threats of his own and portrays himself more than
ready to back them up. A casual reference to biting off the nose of a fellow slave "with whom I got a fighting" identifies Grimes as a no-holds-
barred brawler, a ready match for any man who might take him on.

Douglass depicts his famous battle with Edward Covey in the 1845 *Narrative* as largely a pushing and shoving match, in which the slave prudently deploys just enough resistance to defend himself against the slave breaker's attempts to throttle him. Grimes is a good deal earthier and more aggressive. Schooled "in old Virginia style, (which generally consists in gouging, biting and butting)," Grimes fights multiple antagonists, including white overseers and black slave drivers—"Oh, how much have I suffered from these black drivers!"—who try to force his obedience. When fighting isn't an option, Grimes resorts to wilier deceptions—including passing for white to outwit the Savannah guard—to gain the upper hand over whites and blacks alike. In their narratives, Moses Roper, William Wells Brown, and James W. C. Pennington offer up pious apologies for the tricks they devised to escape punishments and, sometimes, slavery itself.[28] Although Grimes assures his reader that as a slave "I would not lie nor steal," he was not above deceiving whites for his own benefit, nor does he express the slightest regret for having done so.

For the sadistic whites who devised fiendish torture to punish him for his incessant escape attempts, Moses Roper professed a forgiving regard: "I bear no enmity even to the slave-holders but regret their delusions."[29] Grimes's narrative, however, lodges lasting complaints against many of the whites he encountered in the South. He bears a special grudge toward the wife of his first master, William Gibbons Stuart, whose hatred, either because of jealousy or because the light-skinned slave boy was also Mrs. Stuart's first cousin, brought him many harsh beatings before he had reached the age of ten. "Young as I was then, I can yet remember her cruelty with emotions of indignation that almost drove me to curses. She is dead, thank God, and if I ever meet her again, I hope I shall know her." Clearly, William Grimes was not one to forgive or forget.[30] He singles out one of the floggings his mistress told her overseer to administer: "It seems as though I should not forget this flogging when I die; it grieved my soul beyond the power of time to cure. I should not have been alive now if I had remained a slave, for I would have resisted with my life." It is not so much Grimes's espousal of violent resistance that makes this passage notable as his admission that his "soul" had been "grieved" by this treatment in ways that the passage of decades had not ameliorated. He will carry his bitterness beyond the grave, hoping in the next world to settle accounts with a woman whom "I must call her brute."

One rarely finds the celebrated slave narratives of Roper, Douglass, Brown, or Bibb exposing and probing emotional extremes of this sort, especially when they draw attention to the narrator's own psychic wounds. Grimes's African American literary successors, along with their white antislavery sponsors and editors, tended to follow a more self-deflecting script in writing about the horrors of slavery. This unofficial script evolved as antislavery leaders such as William Lloyd Garrison (who wrote the preface to Douglass's 1845 *Narrative*) and the societies they founded (Garrison's American Anti-Slavery Society published both Douglass's *Narrative* and Brown's *Narrative*) appropriated the slave narrative in the late 1830s and the 1840s. Working from this unofficial script, white sponsors and editors felt that slave narrators could do more good for the antislavery cause by assuming the role of eyewitness rather than I-witness. Writers of the slave narrative were urged to focus on the evils of the institution of slavery rather than on their own individuality either in slavery or in freedom. Reviewers often praised those slave narratives in which the injustices of the institution were presented, deposition-like, in a calm, matter-of-fact, quasi-objective fashion, the more to convince readers that the once-enslaved narrator was unbiased, truthful, and trustworthy.[31]

Many of the great slave narratives of the 1840s and 1850s echo Grimes's unsparing indictment of the ways enslavement injured and oppressed black people physically, emotionally, and spiritually. But Grimes wrote his 1825 narrative well *before* the advent of the abolitionist crusade in the North, which most scholars trace to the publication of David Walker's militantly black nationalist *Appeal* in 1829 and the first issue of Garrison's uncompromising antislavery newspaper, the *Liberator*, on January 1, 1831, in Boston. The *Life of William Grimes, the Runaway Slave* appeared before Garrison had even announced publicly his opposition to slavery; before the first African American newspaper, *Freedom's Journal*, appeared in 1827; before the slave boy Frederick Douglass could read the word "abolitionist"; before northern states such as New York and New Jersey outlawed slavery within their borders. By 1855, when Grimes printed the second edition of his *Life*, the antislavery movement was in its heyday in the North. Yet there is no evidence that the movement, even after championing fugitive slave writers such as Douglass, Brown, Bibb, and a dozen others, took cognizance of Grimes's pioneering role in launching the fugitive slave narrative.

Unconnected to any known antislavery or manumission group in the 1820s or thereafter, Grimes seems to have been either unaware of or indifferent to the modes of personal testimony that informed slave narratives both before and after his experimental text. He repeatedly identifies himself, especially in the 1825 *Life*, as a lone battler and solitary survivor in a world in which few can be trusted. Calling himself "a praying soul," Grimes acknowledges a sporadic personal relationship to his God, but rarely in slavery does he seem the actual beneficiary of God's grace, let alone justice. In Grimes's autobiography God is invoked far more often in blasphemous obscenities uttered by whites than in any form of pious discourse. About the only times Grimes calls on God are when his back is against the wall, when no one can possibly forestall a severe beating or provide comfort on the eve of sale to a new master. In Connecticut, Grimes recalls one (typically) solitary occasion when he asked God whether it was his "duty...to go back to my master." Grimes's conclusion—that God delivered him from slavery as God had delivered the Hebrews "out of the land of Egypt"—rehearses a well-worn analogy in African American culture followed by a platitude that sounds more perfunctory than heartfelt: "Therefore, if we trust in God, we need have no fear of the greatest trials."

Grimes's greatest trial was "the cup of slavery" from which he daily imbibed "the bitterest dregs ever mingled in it." "Yet, under the consolations of religion, my fortitude never left me." Perhaps—but readers of the *Life* will be hard put to find more than one or two instances when Grimes actually sought or found "the consolations of religion," especially during his enslavement. The language of bitterness appears much more often in the *Life of William Grimes* than any words of religious consolation.

Some of the most vivid episodes in the *Life* recount Grimes's consultations with fortune-tellers, his humiliations under the spell of a witch, and his dreadful encounters with a ghost. The author is neither ashamed to admit nor intent on explaining away the power that a variety of threatening supernatural forces held over him. Later slave narratives cite hoodoo practices and soothsaying among slaves, but autobiographers such as Douglass and Brown were quick to distance themselves from such "superstition," thereby reassuring their white Protestant readership of their Christian orthodoxy and freedom from African heathenism.[32] Sharing little of the God-centeredness and even less of the Christian commitment professed by Brace, Bayley, Roper, Douglass, Bibb, and Pennington,[33] Grimes's autobiography attests to the narrator's lingering, unreformed interstitial spiritual condition, one foot in Western piety and the other in what Douglass called "the black art" and folk "superstition." No doubt like many slaves, Grimes was a "praying soul" to whom "the consolations of religion" provided limited comfort and assurance in an unpredictable world of terrifyingly inexplicable and malevolent forces, natural and supernatural. To people placed in such a situation—consider Frankee, the menacing slave woman Grimes accuses of being a "witch"[34]—any means of harnessing power and gaining leverage during the ceaseless strife of slavery, whether through prayer, worship, divination, or conjuration, must have seemed well worth trying.

Probably in his sixties Grimes finally joined a Methodist church in New Haven. Through most of his life, however, his lack of firm communion with God is matched by his tenuous ties to earthly community, whether black or white, North or South. A frequent theme in the *Life* is the narrator's friendlessness and loneliness. Even in his 1855 conclusion, he admits that after having established a profitable barbershop in Fairfield, Connecticut, "I ought to have been contented, but I wasn't, and again was on the move." This statement could serve as an epigraph for the entire story of Grimes's life in the North. By maintaining his innocent persecution by perfidious slaves, cruel masters and mistresses, and unscrupulous employers, Grimes sounds a bit like Brace, Bayley, and White, all of whom affiliate their lives to that of a Christian pilgrim seeking redemption according to God's calling and in obedience to his Providence. Grimes's worldview, however, provides little in the way of a spiritual framework to explain or justify his rootless, scuffling, often hand-to-mouth existence, riven with cruel reversals and transient fulfillment. For the famous fugitive slave narrators of the mid-nineteenth century, the attainment of freedom provides a redemptive perspective on the slave past along with a sense of hope and purpose for the future in freedom. But in 1825, Grimes could not espouse any such perspective on his past or his future. His 1855 autobiography makes, at best, a gesture toward forgiveness and hope in the end, but this hardly counterbalances the prevailing mood of loss and resentment permeating the *Life* as a whole.

Grimes's refusal to portray himself as blessed by the attainment of freedom points to what is surely the most remarkable and instructive difference between his singular version of the fugitive slave experience and what was immortalized by the Frederick Douglass school of the slave narrative in the 1840s and 1850s. Freedom did not redeem William Grimes, because, as his story startlingly testifies, the author could not recommend unreservedly life in the North as compared to life in the South. In fact, Grimes could not even urge that other slaves follow his example and run away to the North.

The more that Grimes reveals about his life in the North, the more ironically pointless his flight to freedom seems. Perhaps this is one reason that the later narratives of Roper, Douglass, Brown, Bibb, and Pennington concentrate so much on their authors' experience of slavery and their intrepid escapes to the North or England. Little is said in the classic slave narrative about the aftermath of the flight from bondage except to document a few of the high points of the self-emancipated former slave's career. Typically freedom in the Douglass school of slave narrative consists of noting the narrator's successful establishment of a new identity (often by renaming himself), his new personal commitments (in particular, marriages sanctioned by clergy and law), his respectable employment (freely selected, not coerced), and his dedication to reform work highlighted by antislavery activism (culminating in the writing of the narrative itself). Retailing these indicators of triumphant transition from enslavement to freedom assured white readers that fugitive slaves could and would become socially, economically, and spiritually integrated into the North. As a variation on the American success story, the narratives of Douglass and his school belie the charge of proslavery advocates and northern Negrophobes that without a master to control and direct them, blacks in freedom would soon revert to savagery at worst or dependency at best.

The *Life of William Grimes* tallies few of the milestones of self-fulfillment and communal integration that the heroic fugitives of later narratives inevitably pass on their upward journey in freedom. Grimes lets his

reader know that he had a name in slavery (Theo) different from the
one he was born with, but he doesn't suggest that he rejoiced over the
freedom to name himself once he got to the North. Grimes mentions
his marriage to "a plain looking girl in New Haven," but his suspicions
of women—"the generality of girls are sluttish, though my wife is
not"—and his resentment over having to convince the white minister
who married him that his betrothal was sincere dominate this part of
his story, to the exclusion of his even naming the woman who wed
him.[35] Although most of the famous mid-century fugitive slave narrators reported their ascension to white-collar status as professional ora-
tors, editors, ministers, and, of course, authors, William Grimes, like
the vast majority of African Americans who lived above the Mason-
Dixon line, found no way out of the hustling working class after he
got to freedom. Trying pretty much anything that would turn a profit,
from quarrying stone and cutting wood to dressing hair and peddling
lottery tickets in his old age, Grimes refers to himself as a perpetual
"poor man" throughout his account of his experience in the North.
To be sure, he manages to snatch occasional success from a short-lived
venture or two, but quarrels, fights, lawsuits, and threats keep him on
the defensive most of the time, on a treadmill of survival. The occasional sympathizer from the white upper class puts in a good word for
him once in a while, but he seems to have no community to turn to for
consistent support.

After only one week of freedom, the fugitive slave admits that he
"began to repent that I had ever come away from Savannah." Completing the 1825 version of his *Life*, Grimes pens the most damning critique
of so-called freedom in the North ever recorded in an antebellum slave
narrative:

> I would advise no slave to leave his master. If he runs away,
> he is most sure to be taken: if he is not, he will ever be in the
> apprehension of it; and I do think there is no inducement for a
> slave to leave his master and be set free in the Northern States.
> I have had to work hard; I have been often cheated, insulted,
> abused and injured; yet a black man, if he will be industrious
> and honest, can get along here as well as anyone who is poor
> and in a situation to be imposed on.

The 1855 expanded edition of the *Life* does not retract or modify a word of this. The conclusion promises not "to rake up old affairs," but it still identifies the author as one of the "poor and friendless" and, in an oblique but definite allusion to the infamous 1850 Fugitive Slave Act, reiterates that, even in 1855, he *still* is "not entirely free from apprehension, even in this land of liberty."

Thus the great irony of the first fugitive slave narrative in African American literature is that it counsels the slave who might read it *not* to attempt an escape from slavery. Given what Grimes knew of chattel slavery, what could have caused him almost to disavow the defining decision of his life? Clearly Grimes did not issue his warning out of any nostalgia for slavery. What he went through in the South provided ample justification for his own flight to the North. Nor can anyone read the *Life* without feeling how deeply opposed to human bondage the author was. Nevertheless, despite all he had suffered in slavery, Grimes would not recommend anyone's following his example—unless he is willing to accept the irrefutable fact that although an "industrious" and "honest" black man "can get along here," he should never expect to attain more than "anyone who is poor and in a situation to be imposed on."

This canny diagnosis of the North as a place where class, even more than color, determines a person's fate helps us understand why Grimes portrayed himself both in 1825 and in 1855 primarily as a "poor man," not a Negro. Life in the North had taught the former slave that honesty, industry, and all the other virtues extolled by the young Republic availed a poor man (of any color) little. His poverty and powerlessness gave those with money and influence a freedom that the poor man could never wield, the freedom to impose on the poor and get away with it. From southern slavery one might escape, but from the freedom to be imposed on and exploited there was, for the northern poor, no escape. Thus "to be set free in the Northern States" could be paradoxically more exploitative and humiliating than to be enslaved in the South.

Which was the preferable alternative? Grimes refused to say, although he had seen and lived both sides of the dilemma and was more willing to acknowledge it than any slave narrator before or after him. Perhaps Grimes felt that there was ultimately no alternative, no way out. But it is just as likely that he felt the only way out was to *speak* out, which he did not once but twice, in his rough, unapologetic eloquence. If few listened and even fewer followed his bold example, it is all the more important now that William Grimes be granted a full hearing as well as the credit for honesty and literary individualism long his due.

—William L. Andrews

LIFE OF WILLIAM GRIMES,

THE RUNAWAY SLAVE,

BROUGHT DOWN TO

THE PRESENT TIME. WRITTEN

BY HIMSELF. NEW HAVEN:

PUBLISHED BY

THE AUTHOR. 1855.

To the Public

THOSE who are acquainted with the subscriber, he presumes will readily purchase his history. Those who are not, but wish to know who Grimes is, and what is his history, he would inform them, generally, that he is now living in Litchfield, Connecticut,[1] that he is about forty years of age, that he is married to a black woman, and passes for a negro, though three parts white; that he was born in a place in Virginia, has lived in several different States, and been owned by ten different masters; that about ten years since, he ran away, and came to Connecticut, where, after six years, he was recognized by some of his former master's friends, taken up, and compelled to purchase his freedom with the sacrifice of all he had earned. That his history is an account of his fortune, or rather of his suffering, in all these various situations, in which he has seen, heard, and felt, not a little.

To those who still think the book promises no entertainment, he begs leave to suggest another motive why they should purchase it. To him who has feeling, the condition of a slave, under any possible circumstances, is painful and unfortunate, and will excite the sympathy of all who have any. Such was my condition for more than thirty years, and in circumstances not only painful, but often intolerable. But after having tasted the sweets of liberty, (embittered, indeed, with constant apprehension,) and after having, by eight years labor and exertion, accumulated about a thousand dollars, then to be stripped of all these hard earnings and turned pennyless upon the world with a family, and to purchase freedom, this gives me a claim upon charity, which, I presume, few possess, and I think, none will deny. Let any one suppose himself a husband and father, possessed of a house, home, and livelihood: a stranger enters that house; before his children, and in fair daylight, puts the chain on his leg, where it remains till the last cent of his property buys from avarice and cruelty, the remnant of a life, whose best years had been spent in misery! Let any one imagine this, and think what I have felt.

WILLIAM GRIMES.
Litchfield, October 1st, 1824.

1. A large settlement in northwestern Connecticut. When Grimes first published his narrative in 1825, Litchfield was one of the state's leading commercial and cultural towns.

Life of William Grimes

I WAS born in the year 1784, in J——, County of King George,[2] Virginia, in a land boasting its freedom, and under a government whose motto is Liberty and Equality. I was yet born a slave. My father, ——,[3] was one of the most wealthy planters in Virginia. He had four sons; two by his wife, one, myself, by a slave of Doct. Steward, and another by his own servant maid.[4] In all the Slave States the children follow the condition of their mother; so that, although in fact, the son of ——, I was in law, a bastard and slave, and owed by Doct. Steward.[5] My father was a wild sort of man, and very much feared by all his neighbors. I recollect he shot a man by the name of Billy Hough,[6] through the arm, who came to my master's and staid. He was, however, finally taken up and committed to Fredricksburg jail, for shooting Mr. Gallava, a gentleman of that county.[7] He refused, however, to be taken, until a military force was called out. Then he gave up, went to jail, was tried and acquitted on the ground of insanity.[8]

Doct. Steward's house was about a mile from my father's, where I went frequently, to carry newspapers, &c. He always used to laugh and talk with me, and send me to the kitchen to get something to eat. I also at those times saw and played with his other children. My

2. Approximately seventy miles south of Washington, D.C., and bordered by the Potomac and Rappahannock rivers, with the Chesapeake Bay at its foot.

3. Benjamin Grymes, Jr. (1756–1804), a lieutenant and later captain in the Revolutionary War, was evidently a longtime neighbor and family friend of George Washington. See Liza Lawrence, *The Vistas at Eagle's Nest* (Fredericksburg, VA: Fredericksburg Press, 1969), 7–8.

4. William Fitzhugh (1780–1830), Benjamin (1785–1828), and George Nicholas (1787–1853) were the sons of Benjamin Grymes and his wife, Ann Nicholas. Benjamin's son by his "servant maid" has yet to be determined.

5. Probably William Gibbons Stuart, M.D. (1750–97).

6. William Hooe of King George, Virginia. The shooting was covered by the *Virginia Gazette* and *Richmond and Manchester Advertiser* on August 11, 1794.

7. Robert Galloway, a merchant in Fredericksburg.

8. Benjamin Grymes was acquitted of the murder of Robert Galloway on the grounds of insanity.

brother, the mulatto, was sent to school, and I believe had his freedom when he grew up. My father, I have no doubt, would have bought and freed me, if I had not been sold and taken off while he was in jail. I supposed my father would have been hung; and whether wealth and powerful friends procured his escape, I know not. It is, however, a sufficient commentary upon that event, and upon my fortune, that I then thought and now speak on the subject with indifference. He died at his own house in J——, about the year 1804. That he suffered his blood to run in the veins of a slave, is the only reflection I would cast upon his memory, which is just none at all in the Slave States. He was a very brave man, I reckon; and when it was attempted to take him, armed his slaves, and would never have been taken alive, if some of his friends had not persuaded him to yield quietly. Mr. Gallava was passing my father's when my father met him, and asked him to stop; he said, no, he could not. My father then drew his pistol and shot him dead. Mr. Gallava's servant came directly to Doctor Steward and gave the alarm.

My father inherited the house and plantation where he lived from his father, who was a man of considerable notoriety, and, I believe, both respected and beloved. His character I cannot give. His name, however, has been embalmed by the muses, and lives in song; he being the very person on whom that famous song called, "Old Grimes," was written. The lines are as follows:
TUNE—"John Gilpin was a citizen."

> Old Grimes is dead.— That good old man
> We ne'er shall see him more;
> He used to wear a long black coat,
> All button'd down before.

> His heart was open as the day;
> His feelings all were true;
> His hair was some inclin'd to gray—
> He wore it in a queue.

> Whene'er was heard the voice of pain
> His breast with pity burn'd—
> The large, round head upon his cane,
> From ivory was turn'd.

Thus, ever prompt at pity's call,
He knew no base design—
His eyes were dark, and rather small;
His nose was aquiline.

He liv'd at peace with all mankind,
In friendship he was true;
His coat had pocket holes behind—
His pantaloons were blue.

Unharm'd—the sin which earth pollutes,
He pass'd securely o'er:
And never wore a pair of boots,
For thirty years or more.

But poor *Old Grimes* is now at rest,
Nor fears misfortune's frown;
He had a double-breasted vest—
The stripes ran up and down.

He modest merit sought to find,
And pay it its desert:
He had no malice in his mind—
No ruffles on his shirt.

His neighbors he did not abuse,
Was sociable and gay;
He wore large buckles in his shoes,
And chang'd them every day.

His knowledge hid from public gaze,
He did not bring to view—
Nor make a noise town-meeting days,
As many people do.

His worldly goods he never threw
In trust to fortune's chances;
But liv'd (as all his brothers do)
In easy circumstances.

Thus, undisturb'd by anxious care,
His peaceful moments ran;

And ev'ry body said he was
A fine old gentleman.

Good people all, give cheerful thought
To Grimes' memory:
As doth his cousin, ESEK SHORT,
Who made this poetry.

Such, according to Esek Short[9], was the character of my grandfather; and, if it is impartially given, I think the family has degenerated. One would think, though, Mr. Short admired old Grimes' virtues more than he lamented his death.

Doct. Steward kept me until I was ten years old. I used to ride behind the carriage to open gates, and hold his horse. He was very fond of me, and always treated me kindly. This made my old mistress,[10] his wife, hate me; and when she caught me in the house, she would beat me until I could hardly stand. Young as I was then, I can yet remember her cruelty with emotions of indignation that almost drove me to curses. She is dead, thank God, and if I ever meet her again, I hope I shall know her.

When I was ten years of age, Col. William Thornton[11] came down from the mountains, in Culpepper County, to buy negroes, and he came to my master's house, who was his brother-in-law, and seeing me, thought me a smart boy. He asked my master what he would take for me: he replied, he thought I was worth £60. Col. Thornton immediately offered £65, and the bargain was made. The next morning I started with him for Culpepper. It grieved me to see my mother's tears at our separation. I was a heart-broken child, although too young to realize the afflictions of a tender mother, who was also a slave, the hopes of freedom for her already lost; but I was compelled to go and leave her.

9. From the middle of the eighteenth century, the Short family owned "Machodoc Dam," a large piece of land marked with stone monuments, bearing the name "John Short 1754" and bordering Eagle's Nest.

10. Mary Fitzhugh Stuart was the wife of William Gibbons Stuart and the first cousin of Benjamin Grymes.

11. Colonel William Thornton (1745–1818), brother-in-law of William Gibbons Stuart, was present at the reading of Stuart's will. Thornton was married to Martha Stuart, daughter of John Stuart.

After two days travel on horseback, we arrived at my new master's plantation, which was called Montpelier.[12] After residing there a few weeks, my mistress, finding me an honest servant boy, I was then intrusted with all the keys, which made some of the other servants jealous, who had, when in the situation which I held, pilfered from the stores entrusted to their care, for the purpose of giving to their acquaintances and relations; one in particular, my mistress's head servant and seamstress, who had as many children as my mistress, and who were then working on the plantation. They fared much harder there than they would in my situation. She tried every art she could invent to set my master and mistress against me. As I had to make the coffee every morning in the nursery, where this servant, whose name was Patty, sat sewing, she would, when I was out, often take medicine from the cupboard, and put it in the coffee; and her object in doing this, was to compel me to go on the plantation, and have one of her children in my place. But as I was a poor friendless boy, without any connexions or inducements to that, if I had been disposed, my mistress was determined to keep me in my present situation.

But the favorable opinion my mistress had of my integrity (which was correct) has cost me many a severe flagellation, in the manner which I will now relate. I had always made the coffee to the satisfaction of my mistress, until one morning my young master, George Thornton, after taking two or three sips at it, observed, this coffee has a particular taste; and Doct. Hawes,[13] whom I shall hereafter mention, being then at the table, observed the same, adding that it tasted as if some medicine had been put in it. Upon this remark of the Doctor, my mistress rose up from the table and went to the cupboard where the medicine was kept; and after examining said, "Here is where he has just taken it from this morning." My master then rose up in anger, and took me behind the ice-house, and whipped me severely in the following manner: First, he caused me

12. The Montpelier estate was part of Culpepper County until 1833, when Rappahannock County incorporated Culpepper County.

13. Aylett Hawes (1768–1833) was a member of the Virginia House of Delegates from 1802 to 1806 and was a representative in the United States Congress from 1811 to 1817. He returned to his medical practice in Rappahannock County in 1817 and married Fanny Thornton, the eldest daughter of Col. William Thornton.

to be what they call horsed up, by being raised upon the shoulders of another slave, and the slave to confine my hands around his breast; in this situation they gave me about forty or fifty lashes; they whipped me until I had hardly any feeling in me. The crime was sufficiently deserving the punishment, but for a young boy who had tried and exerted himself to the utmost to give good satisfaction to his master, mistress, and all the family, never intending to injure any other servant, but rather participate in their wrongs, and render assistance if it could lawfully be done; and all for the malicious temper and disposition of this same Patty, it was too much for me to bear. It indeed sometimes happened, that every morning I was taken and whipped severely, for this very act of that malicious (I must call her brute,) when I was entirely innocent. There, without friends, torn from the arms of my mother, who has since died in slavery, not being allowed to see me, her only son, during her last illness: (I knew of course she would suffer while confined and unable to help herself, and no one willing to help her that could be allowed to see her,) this, together with my sufferings, is sufficient to convince my readers, that any boy of my age would endeavor to find, and also improve an opportunity to clear themselves from the house of bondage.

Doct. Hawes, aforementioned, was present at the time I was whipped on account of the coffee, and advised my master not to whip me any more, as he thought I could not bear it much longer. He was my master's son-in-law, and a member of Congress, and married my master's eldest daughter. He did not whip me any more at that time, after the advice of the Doctor. Oftentimes, my mistress would have me make the coffee in the dining room, before her. At such times Patty had no opportunity for putting in the drugs, and the coffee was then good. I was satisfied in my own mind, that as she was the overseer of the house, and her husband of the plantation, there being about ten or fifteen servants about the house, and no one of them allowed to interfere with this business in which I was employed, that it must be through her machinations which she employed to injure me and get me severely flogged.

One time they had what they call a spell,[14] on the plantation, at which all the servants were compelled to turn out and assist in hoing

---

14. A set of persons each taking a turn of work in sequence in order to relieve the others.

corn. I then requested my master to let me go and assist them. He finally consented, and I went. After working there two days, they requested me to come back in the house again, but I refused; and in order that I should be punished for refusing to return, my master and mistress consented to my staying, thinking that my labor and fare would be so much harder that I would willingly return; but the fear of making the coffee and of the whipping I should receive, induced me still to refuse to return; although at the same time I longed to return on account of my food, (as did the children of Israel to the flesh pots of Egypt.[15]) Patty and her husband were then better satisfied, for they had me just where they wanted me; that is, out of the house into the field, where I suffered everything but death itself.

When I was in waiting at the house, Maj. Jones, brother-in-law to my master, saw me waiting about the house, and thinking me a smart active boy to wait about the house, asked my master if he would sell me. He refused, saying he wanted me to wait on his son, William Thornton, jr., who was studying with Lawyer Thompson, near Culpepper Court House, as soon as he should go into business for himself. So I was not sold this time.

I remained on the plantation about two years, under a black over-seer by the name of Voluntine, who punished me repeatedly, to make me perform more labor than the rest of the boys. My master then pro-cured another overseer, a white man, by the name of Coleman Thead; he treated us somewhat better than old Voluntine, but he was very severe, and flogged me severely several times, for almost nothing. The overseers have an unlimited control over the slaves on the plantation, and exercise their authority in the most tyranical manner. I was one day at work on the plantation, with nothing on but my shirt, when the overseer (Thead) came to me, threatening to whip me, and caught hold of me for that purpose. I clinched him and told him that if he struck me, I would inform my master about his riding a favorite horse

15. Exodus 16:3: "And the children of Israel said unto them, would to God we had died by the hand of the Lord in the land of Egypt, when we sat by the flesh pots, and when we did eat bread to the full; for ye have brought us forth into this wilderness, to kill this whole assembly with hunger."

without my master's consent; that my master had already enquired of me why the horse grew so poor, but I would not tell him; the fear of detection induced him to let me go, telling me to be a good boy, and he would not flog me. I worked under this overseer about nine months, when he left us and went to Georgia.

I then worked under old Voluntine again, for about six months, when my master engaged a new overseer by the name of *Burrows:* he was more severe than either of the former. After working with him some time, he set us to making fence, and would compel us to run with the rails on our backs, whipping us all the time most unmercifully. This hard treatment continuing for some time, I at length resolved to run away. I accordingly repaired to the cabin of a slave called *Planter George,* and informed him that I intended to run away the next morning. I asked him for an old jacket and some meal, both of which he promised to give me. I then baked what meal I had for my supper, and went to sleep. Old George immediately repaired to the house of the overseer and informed him of my intention to run away in the morning. The overseer came directly to the cabin and sent in George to question me, while he should listen without. George asked me if I intended to run away provided he would give me the jacket and some meal; being partly asleep I answered that I did not know. He repeated the question several times and still received the same answer. The overseer then hallooed out, "Hey, you son of a bitch, you are going to run away, are you? I'll give it to you; bring him out here." So they brought me out and horsed me upon the back of Planter George, and whipped me until I could hardly stand, and then told me if I did not run away he would whip me three times a day, and make me carry three rails to one all day. In this manner do the overseers impose on their planters and compel their slaves to run away, by cruel treatment.

The next morning came, and I knew not what to do. If I went to the field, I was sure to be whipped, and to run away I did not like to. However, like most, I presume in my situation, I chose the latter alternative, so away I ran for the mountain. I passed close by the field where my young master, Philip Thornton, was shooting. His gun burst and blew off part of his thumb. I crept along under the fence, and got to the mountains, where I staid until night: then I began to be hungry, and thought I would go to some of the neighbors to get something to eat.

I went to Mr. Pallam's and asked for some tobacco seed for my master for an excuse, and staid there all night, I got some corn bread for my supper, and picked up a little about the kitchen for the next day.

The next morning, I went to the mountains and staid till night again, when I went down to Mr. Pallam's to get something to eat, pretending that I had come on an errand from my master. Mr. Pellam immediately seized me and called to Daniel to bring the hame strings.[16] He had been down to my master's that day and they told him I had gone off, and if I came there again, to take me, which he did, and would have carried me home that night, but his wife persuaded him to wait till morning. I was then put under the care of old Daniel. Mr. Pallam told me if I ran away from him he would catch me with his dogs, for they would track me any where. Daniel took me to his hovel, and for greater security took away my shoes.

I lay peaceable till near morning, when the fear of my master came over me again, and I wished to get away. I begged old Daniel to let me go out, under pretence of necessity, but he refused. He finally gave me one of his shoes, and I went to the door to look out. It was just the dawn of day. I had been waiting the cock crowing all night, and it was now time to go if I went at all. The ground was covered with a light snow. I gave a jump and Daniel after me, but my step was as light as the snow flake, and the last glimpse I had of Daniel showed him prostrate over a log. I escaped to a corn field in sight of my master's house, and secreted myself in an old log which I had picked out before. While in the log I fell asleep, and dreamed they had caught and was tying me to be whipped; and such was my agony that I awoke, from a dream, indeed, but to reality not less painful.

I staid in that place about three days, when I became so pinched with hunger, that I thought I might as well be whipped to death as to starve; so I concluded to give myself up, if I could get to my master before the overseer should get me. In that I succeeded. They gave me something to eat, and Doct. Hawes, my master's son-in-law, who was at the house,

16. A hame was a curved piece of wood that formed the collar of a draught horse. The hame strings are leather straps with buckles used to fasten the hames onto the collar.

advised them not to whip me. My master asked me what made me go off: I told him the cruelty of the overseer. He then told the overseer not to whip me again without his knowledge. I was so hungry that they were afraid to give me as much as I wanted, lest I should kill myself. Not long after, however the overseer came into the field where we were at work, and after trying to find some fault, whipped us all around. This was the first time he had done it since my master told him not; but I dare not tell my master, for if I did, the overseer would whip me for that. If it were not for our hopes, our hearts would break; we poor slaves always cherish hopes of better times. We are human beings, sensible of injuries, and capable of gratitude towards our masters. This overseer whipped me a great many times before I escaped from his hands.

Shortly after this I recollect my master came home late at night, and getting off his horse, got entangled, and would have fallen if I had not been near, and caught him; and being a very large man, the fall might have injured him very much, nay, killed him. Afterwards, when he was angry with me, I could sometimes appease him somewhat by hinting this to him.

There is a holiday which our master gave us, called Easter Sunday or Monday. On one of those days I asked my young master, Stuart Thornton, to let me go and see Miss Jourdine, a mulatto girl who was brought up with me and sold by Doct. Steward to Mr. Glassel. It was eight years before that when I saw her last. She was then a beautiful girl. I cannot describe the emotions of pleasure with which her presence filled my bosom, nor forget the hour when fate parted us forever. I presume the heart and the feelings of an illiterate peasant or an ignorant slave, are as susceptible and as ardent as those of men more enlightened, at least when warmed and excited by the influence of female attractions. The last look of a woman whom you know loves you, which is given through tears and with a consciousness that you are leaving her forever, troubles my heart beyond any thing I have since experienced. My young master did not like me to go, but I did.

On the way my bosom burned and my heart almost leaped from me, as I thought on this girl. I felt as though I could, unarmed, have flogged half a dozen lions if they had crossed my path. I did not find her at Mr. Glassel's, she having been sold to Mr. Jourdine, who had bought her and kept her for his wife; but I did not return without seeing her.

One of the Miss Glassels sent a book to my young mistress, to whom I presented it on my return. She asked me where I had been: I told her I had been to see Miss Jourdine. And because I called the girl Miss instead of Betty,[17] my young mistress was extremely angry with me, and said she would have me whipped in the morning.

In the morning Burrows, the overseer, came after me to Aaron's cabin, where I staid. As I came towards the house, my master came out, The little rascal, says he, had the impertinence to call that wench Miss Jourdine to his mistress; take him and give it to him. So they took me and tied me on a bench, and as soon as they began to whip, I would slip out from the rope, until my master told the overseer to horse me upon another's back, and after he had whipped me a while to stop and let me rest; for he said he wanted to whip me about a month. They began to whip again in a few minutes, though not so hard, and kept it up three or four hours; I begging all the while to be forgiven, and promising to offend no more. I was so weak after this, I could hardly stand, but they would not have got me to whip if it had not snowed, and prevented me from running away to the mountain. My master gave me many very severe floggings; but I had rather be whipped by him than the overseer, and especially the black overseers. Oh, how much have I suffered from these black drivers!

Sometime during this year, my master's son, George, wanted me to wait on him. He came to the field where I was at work, to see me. I had been fighting with Moses, and had cut off my hair as close as possible, for the purpose of having the advantage. Seeing this, he refused to take me, I looked so bad. So I was obliged to remain in the field and live on my peck of meal[18] a week. Colonel Thornton was a severe master, and he made his slaves work harder than any one about there, and kept them poorer. Sometimes we had a little meat, or fish, but not often anything more than our peck of meal. We used to steal meat whenever we could get a chance; and such was my craving for it, that if the

---

17. A slave girl, "Betty," appears in the 1798 inventory and appraisal of Doctor William G. Stuart's estate. By that time, Col. William Thornton had already purchased William Grimes from Stuart.

18. A peck is equivalent to eight quarts or approximately nine liters.

punishment had been death, I could not have resisted the temptation. How much I suffered, I will not pretend to say; but I recollect one Saturday I had been to work hard all day: in the evening, I found, back of the garden, some hog's entrails which had been thrown out a few days before. I was so hungry for meat, that I took these guts, washed them, and put them into a skillet and boiled them. I then wet some corn meal in cold water, put it in the ashes, and made a fire over it. After it had baked, I mixed it with the guts and eat it; but before morning I was so much swollen that I liked to have died. When any of the hogs died, we always eat them. But we did not wait for pigs and geese to die of old age, when we could get a chance to steal them. Steal? Yes, steal them. Why, I have been so hungry for meat that I could have eat my mother.

One instance of cruelty from my mistress I can never forget. It was my turn to beat homony[19] that night. So I began at dark and beat most all night. Having been at work hard all day, before morning I was so hungry that I took and fanned the chaff and husks from the corn I was beating, wet it up with water, and baked it, and this without one grain of salt or fat. I had worked as hard as I could, and beat the homony as I thought sufficiently. About an hour before day, I lay down and went to sleep. In the morning, my mistress sent to the overseer to give me a severe whipping, for she said the homony was not beat quite enough, though very good. Notwithstanding I had worked all night as hard as I could spring, I was taken and flogged. (Homony is a kind of food used at breakfast and dinner. It is made of corn pounded till the skin is all off, then boiled, mashed and fried.) It seems as though I should not forget this flogging when I die; it grieved my soul beyond the power of time to cure. I should not have been alive now if I had remained a slave, for I would have resisted with my life, when I became older, treatment which I have witnessed towards others, from the overseers, and such as I should probably have met with, nay, such as I have received when a boy from overseers.

While I was with Col. William Thornton, a great many of his slaves were taken sick and died. Doct. Hawes married one of Col. Thornton's

19. Hominy is hulled and ground corn boiled with water or milk and often fried.

daughters, Fanny Thornton. My master gave him a tract of land in Culpepper, on which he built himself a house,[20] about a mile from my master's, and came up there to live, from Caroline, Spotsylvania county. We always supposed that some of his slaves poisoned my master's; and I heard one of the servants say, that he saw an old woman of Doct. Hawes' put something like red earth into the bread. Several of the servants in the spinning room died, and after that there was a groaning heard in that room; and I have myself heard the spirits groan in that room. If ever there was a room haunted it was that. I will believe it as long as I have my breath to draw. I slept in the passage, close by the door of my master and mistress. Sometimes when I was as wide awake as I am now, the spirits would unlock the doors, and come up stairs, and trample on me, press me to the floor, and squeeze me almost to death; I should have screamed, but the fear of my master, who would not believe, but would have whipped me, prevented.

There was, not long after this, a great hurricane and earthquake;[21] and I saw the sky part and it looked as red as crimson. The earth shook, and every thing that was on it; and I heard them talk of many thousands who were drowned.

There was, I recollect, at my master's, two gentlemen from Connecticut, Parson Beebe and Doct. Goodsell. They staid there sometime, and it was supposed Doct. Goodsell was courting my young mistress. One of my young masters came on to court with them. I heard them talk about New Haven, but I little thought I should ever see it.

While I was at work under Burrows, the overseer, my master's son, George, returned from Philadelphia, where he had been studying physic. He went to Northumberland County[22] to practice, and took me from the plantation to wait on him. In going to Northumberland, we

---

20. Hawes's house was named the Hawthorn Plantation.

21. Probably a reference to the Great Coastal Hurricane of 1806 (August 21–23), which significantly damaged areas in the Carolinas and coastal Virginia.

22. Known as the "Mother County of the Northern Neck," Northumberland is located on the coast of Chesapeake Bay, situated between the Potomac and Rappahannock rivers.

passed through Leedstown,²³ where I saw my mother and brothers.²⁴ It was, I suppose, ten years since I had seen my mother. She was living with her old mistress, Doct. Steward's former wife, but now married to George Fitchue,²⁵ Doct. Steward being dead. There is nothing in slavery, perhaps, more painful, than the unavoidable separation of parents and children. It is not uncommon to hear mothers say, that they have half a dozen children, but the Lord only knows where they are. Oh! my poor mother! but she is gone, and I presume her skin is now as white as that of her mistress.

Master George hired a house in Northumberland, and I took care of the house when he was gone. I always had been praying to God, ever since I knew what God was; and I thought, like Peter, I had faith. One day, when I was alone in the house, I shut all the doors in the house, and went up into the third story to pray; and just as I entered the room, I saw, to my astonishment, a number of skeletons hanging up about it. It was a terrible sight to me, and I was so frightened that I could not stop. The holes in the skull, where the eyes are, seemed to look right at me. I turned round as slowly and softly as possible, without taking my eyes from them until I shut the door. I have often thought it strange, that a skeleton or a corpse should terrify us, though they might shock our feelings. But my poor heart never walloped so before; and I had never thought our garret was a sepulchre.

My master sent me to Fredericksburg²⁶ to get another doctor to come and help him cut off a woman's thigh. I had helped him once, but I almost fainted. When I had got in town and done my errand, I put out

23. At the time of this narrative, an unincorporated village in Westmoreland Country, thirty miles southeast of Fredericksburg on the Rappahannock River.

24. The identity of Grimes's mother is unknown. Grimes's reference to his "brothers" may denote his white half-brothers, William Fitzhugh, Benjamin, and George Nicholas. Whether Grimes also had siblings from his biological mother is unknown.

25. Doctor Stuart's widow became Mary Fitzhugh Stuart Fitzhugh by taking her cousin George Fitzhugh as her second husband.

26. Fredericksburg is fifty miles south of Washington, D.C., and fifty-five miles north of Richmond, Virginia.

my horse at the tavern, and went into the kitchen, where, who should I find but my old master's cook, Philip. He told me that my brother Benjamin[27] was in town. I went to see him, and told him who I was. He gave me seventy-five cents. With this I went and bought some cake and rum, and drank, not thinking, until I got drunk and fell down in the street. Some of my friends took me up and carried me in, and I slept till most night, when I started for home, and rode with all haste, lest my master should flog me for staying. I pretended to him that I rode slow. However, as I did not let him see the horse he never found out my scrape, and it is well he did not, for if he had, I might not have been here to record it. He was cross to me and I feared him like death. I recollect once his whipping me, after our return from Northumberland, so severely on the naked back, that I carry the stripes to this day, and all because his mother told him that I had been telling his younger brother something that was done when he lived at Northumberland. He gave me once a tumbler of spirits, and made me drink it, which almost killed me. This he did to conceal from my knowledge a scrape which he was going to have, as I supposed. If the cook had not blown tobacco smoke through me, I believe I should have been a corpse before morning.

After staying at Northumberland six or eight months, master George left there, and I went back to his father's plantation—I went sorrowing, too. Master George was going to Philadelphia again, so there was no other place for me but his father's plantation, where I must work all day, and sometimes most all night, with my peck of meal a week, and the hell-hound Burrows to flog me, for he gloried in doing it. One instance in which my master disappointed his savage heart, I remember. He told Burrows to take me down to the stable, tie my legs, put a rail between them, then stretch me up and whip me. While going down to the stable, which was about thirty or forty rods distant, I thought if the order was put in execution, I could not endure it, but must die in the operation. My master and Burrows went forward, and I followed behind. I looked up to heaven and prayed fervently to God to hear my prayer, and grant me relief in this hour of adversity; expecting every moment to

27. Grimes's half-brother Benjamin (1785–1828) was the middle son of Benjamin Grymes and his wife, Ann Nicholas.

be whipped until I could not stand; and *blessed be God* that he turned their hearts before they arrived at the place of destination: for, on arriving there, I was acquitted. God delivered me from the power of the adversary. Blessed be his name, he heard my prayer in the hour of adversity, and delivered me from the enemy. I will here inform my readers, that in the time of going down to the stable, I did not make a feeble attempt to induce my master not to flog me; but put my trust, and offered my prayers to my heavenly Father, who heard and answered them.

On my arriving at the stable, I was surprised to hear my master express himself in terms that I could not reasonably from former treatment expect. He said to me, "go, behave yourself well and you shall not be whipped." In the meantime, Burrows, the overseer, who had stood by wanting and waiting for the privilege of whipping me, stood in suspense and astonishment at the lenity of my master in not having me flogged after he, Burrows, had everything prepared for the purpose; such as a bundle of hickories, ropes to bind me, and a good stout hand to lay it on; ah! and a good resolution.

At one time my master having caused an oven to be built in the yard, for the purpose of baking bread for the negroes, I went there and finding it not quite dry, made impressions with my fingers, such as letters, &c., on it, while the mortar was green on the outside. Gabriel, one of the servants, a son of old Voluntine, was ordered to strip my shirt up and whip me; (the word severely has been so many times used it needs no repetition;) my master stood by to see the thing well executed: and as he thought he did not be severe enough, he ordered me to strip him and perform the same ceremony, which I did. He then ordered Gabriel to try to whip me harder than he did before. Then Gabriel knew what the old man meant, to wit, to whip me as severely as lay in his power, which he effected on the second trial, exerting all his strength and agility to the utmost to make me suffer, only to please his master. This being so often the case, the negro drivers and indeed the slaves, show much less humanity in punishment, than the masters themselves.

Again, while living with my present, or old master, Col. William Thornton, I had the care of some cows, two of which had calves; and I tried to invent some method to get some milk from these cows, to eat my corn bread; but dared not let any person know that I did it, fearing that if I did I should receive a severe whipping. But a stratagem occurred to me. We had gourds growing on the side of the fence. I had often used and seen used, the shell of the gourd for a ladle, or scoup dish, and I took a gourd that was green, and excoriated a part, took out the seeds, &c., and without any further cleansing, I filled it with milk from the cow, and then hid it in the chaff pen. I then went home and baked some bread, and got another gourd and carried there the milk. Being in an open place and it requiring straining, I had nothing at all to strain it through; but being under necessity, I took a part of my shirt tail, which being made of coarse tow cloth, and not having been washed for five or six weeks, I being a poor motherless boy, and no one to wash it but myself, and I all the time kept busy in the field, under the overseer; my shirt was what would be generally termed, full of lice at the time; but as I had no other cloth for straining I made use of that. But when I went to get the milk, the gourd being green, the milk had contracted a bitterness of which no one can judge, unless they have had a trial. I was however driven to the necessity of eating it, or eating my bread dry. I was quite fearful of being taken by old James, a black servant, who was very much respected by master and mistress, although very deceitful, but escaped his vigilance. He died before I began to wait on any of my young masters; and peace be to his soul.

Master George returned from Philadelphia in about a year. He courted his cousin, who lived about six miles from his father's, and married her. His father gave him a plantation, a mile from his own, where I was now placed. My master lived at my wife's father's, intending to move in the spring; this being the fall season. The name of his overseer was Bennet. This Bennet and his mother, had lived on land rented to them by my former master, Col. Thornton. They were then very poor, and secretly bought things from the negroes which they had stolen from my master. This Bennet, having now become overseer, was severe. My master had a servant by his wife's estate called James. I saw Bennet strip off James' shirt, and whip his naked back as if he had been cutting down a tree. I thought what was to be my fate.

One day I was sick and did not go to ploughing. Bennet came after me, and told me he would whip me if I did not. I took up a stick, and told him if he put his hand upon me I would strike him; and marched towards him as bold as a lion. But he knew that I had lived so poor that I had not much strength; and seeing that he did not fear but was in a great rage, I took to my heels. But he caught me, and dragged me up to the negro houses, and called two of them to come and assist him. While they were tying me, I made one pitch at Bennet with my head. I missed him, but he hit me with a club, and knocked me speechless. The blood ran from my mouth and nose very fast. I was then so weak that I could hardly stand; so I gave up, and told the overseer to whip me as much as he pleased, but if he did not whip me to death he should drink sorrow for it. When I was tied, James brought the sticks. I spoke out brave, and said to the overseer, why don't you get some better ones; whip me till your soul is satisfied, but I'll remember every stick. He began to whip, and I counted out loud every stroke. After he had struck me eleven times, he said, if you will say that you are drunk, and hold your peace, I will stop. I said, you might as well whip me to death; for if you don't master will, when he hears of this. But he promised me that if I would hold my tongue, and say nothing about this, he would see that I should not be whipped. He knew that it was for his interest to keep me from exposing their buying things which they knew the slaves had stolen. My master, however, heard something about this scrape, and was going to whip me, but Mr. Bennet interfered, and told him that I was drunk, as I said, and that he had whipped me enough.

I ought, perhaps, to blame slavery more than my master's. The disposition to tyrannize over those under us, is universal; and there is no one who will not occasionally do it. I had too much sense and feeling to be a slave; too much of the blood of my father, whose spirit feared nothing. I was therefore, perhaps, difficult to *govern in the way in which it was attempted.*

I was at this time the property of George Thornton, to whom I was given by his father. Doct. P. T., an older brother, at this time came up from his father's plantation to buy me, which he did. I was then in the ice-house; he called me up, and the moment I saw him my heart leaped for joy. He asked me if I was willing to go and wait on him, as it would be much easier for me than it would to work on the plantation? I answered, yes sir, if you please. He then said he had bought me, and was going to Port Royal,[28] to practice physic, and wanted me to go

---

28. A village twenty miles southeast of Fredericksburg, Virginia, incorporated in 1865.

with him on another horse, carry his portmanteau and wait on him.
He then sent me to the tailor's to get some clothes, and fitted me out
very handsomely. We traveled on to Port Royal, where he went into
practice. I had two horses to take care of.

After remaining there a couple of months, he formed an acquaintance with a young lady, who he afterwards married. After he had
been married one month and four days, his wife died. Soon after that
we returned to his father's plantation in Montpelier. After remaining
there a few days we went on to Frederickstown in Maryland,[29] where
we staid a short time, and returned again to his father's. After a short
stay there, we went to Monticello, and resided at the house of Thomas
Jefferson, formerly President of the United States, for a few weeks.[30]
While we were there he met with his brother-in-law, from Port Royal,
and we returned to that place, when he stayed long enough to settle up
his business, and then went to Richmond, Virginia, to practice physic,
where he had a very good run of business.

After some time, having an opportunity to earn something, I had
laid up a few dollars, and being very fond of having my fortune told,
I was anxious to know whether I should be a free man or not. I went
to an old woman who told fortunes, in order to have her tell mine, a
number of times. She told me that I should be sold to a gentleman,
and be taken to the south. I asked her what kind of a man he was: she
told me his head was white, which I afterwards found to be true, for he
used powder. What she told me proved to be true: she told me he was a
crabbed sort of a man and that I should be severely dealt with. She said
to me, don't you go, your master will not compel you to go, but you
will finally consent to it, and will go. I told her I would not go. She again
told me that I would. I have since thought it strange how this old creature could tell me exactly as it was; but it was so. The man who bought
me was at this time in New York, some hundreds of miles off.

---

29. Fredericktown is located on the Sassafras River in northern Maryland,
approximately thirty miles northwest of Dover, Delaware.

30. Several letters dated from 1814 to 1818 written between Thornton and
Thomas Jefferson survive, but there are no published records of this visit to
Monticello.

Some months after this, one morning as I was busily engaged about the yard, cleaning my master's boots, and doing other work as usual, a gentleman came into the yard at the bell tavern, where my master boarded, and enquired of one of the servants for Doct. Thornton. He told him he did not know where he was, but pointing to me said, there is his servant, sir. He then said to me, are you his servant boy? I answered him that I was. He then told me to go up and tell my master (who was then in bed) that he wanted to see him. I went and told my master there was a gentleman below who wished to see him. He told me to invite him up into his room. I did so and showed him the way up, where I left them together. A short time after this he came down and asked me if I should be willing to go to Savannah with him, provided he should buy me. I told him I did not know where it was. He then told me to go up and see my master. I did so, and he asked me if I wanted to go with that gentleman. I told him I was very well contented to live with him. (He had always treated me perfectly well, we never had any difficulty.) I found that this gentleman had enquired on the road for a good servant, and being informed that my master had one that he would sell, he came to buy me.

My master told me that this gentleman was rich and would be likely to give me my time[31] after a few years, but I did not agree to go still. The gentleman again returned from the eagle tavern to our boarding house, the bell tavern. He then slipped two dollars into my hand and said, here, boy, take this and say you will go; and after a great deal of coaxing and flattering, I finally consented to go, for which I have many a time and often heartily repented. He then went to my master and I followed him. He told him that I had consented to go. My master said he would not force me to go, but if I was willing he would consent to it. Mr. A——, (for that was my new master's name, who was a Jew,) then paid him five hundred dollars. Doct. Thornton then ordered his horse up: he would not stay to see me start, but bade me good bye, and rode off with tears in his eyes.

31. Some owners allowed their slaves to work at a trade outside the master's home. Once paid, the slave was expected to turn over part or, more frequently, all of his wages to his master. In the nineteenth century, to be given one's time also meant to be dismissed from a job or freed from a contract.

I then started with my new master for Savannah,[32] with a carriage and four horses; we traveled about twelve miles the first day. I was dissatisfied with him before I had got two miles. We traveled the next day twenty-five miles, as far as Petersburgh.[33] I was so much dissatisfied with him, that I offered a black man at that place, two silver dollars to take an axe and break my leg, in order that I could not go on to Savannah; but he refused, saying he could tell me a better way. I asked him how? He said run away. I told him I would not run away unless I was sure of gaining my freedom by it. We then traveled on the next day about thirty miles, and put up for the night. I then attempted to break my leg myself. Accordingly I took up an axe, and laying my leg on a log, I struck at it several times with an axe endeavoring to break it, at the same time I put up my fervent prayers to God to be my guide, saying, "if it be thy will that I break my leg in order that I may not go on to Georgia, grant that my blows may take effect; but thy will not mine be done." Finding I could not hit my leg after a number of fruitless attempts, I was convinced by my feelings then, that God had not left me in my sixth trouble, and would be with me in the seventh.[34] Accordingly I tried no more to destroy myself. I then prayed to God, that if it was his will that I should go, that I might willingly. My old master and mistress in Virginia had often threatened to sell me to the negro buyer from Georgia, for any trifling offence, and in order to make me dislike to go there, they would tell me I should have to eat cotton seed and make indigo, and not have corn bread to eat as I did in Virginia.

The next day we went as far as Columbia, in South Carolina.[35] This was Saturday evening. I was quite fatigued, and after taking care of the

---

32. At the time, the second largest city in Georgia, located in the eastern part of the state.

33. Located twenty-five miles south of Richmond.

34. Job 5:19: "He shall deliver thee in six troubles: yea, in seven there shall no evil touch thee."

35. Located 350 miles southwest of Petersburg, Virginia, in the center of South Carolina, Columbia became the state capital in 1786.

horses, I laid myself down in the stable to rest. I soon fell asleep, and slept for an hour or two. My master missing me, and thinking I had run away, made a thorough search for me, but could not find me until I awoke and went into the house. He was very angry with me: he cursed me and asked me where I had been. I told him I had been asleep in the stable. He told me I lied, and that I had attempted to make my escape; threatening to whip me. I told him I had not attempted any thing of the kind; but he would not believe me. Here, again, I was in great trouble. I went to bed and slept as well as I could, which was but little.

The next day we pursued our journey, and nothing of any consequence occurred, different from what had before taken place, until we arrived at Savannah, which was in about six weeks. As we entered the city, we were about to pass a man who had a gun on his shoulder, loaded with shot. It accidentally went off, the contents within a very few inches of me. Here, again, I escaped a wound, if not death. After residing in Savannah for a few months, and perceiving that he grew more severe and inhuman with me every day, I began to despair of ever living with him in peace. I however found some friends in Savannah, after a short time, and they advised me (after being made acquainted with the manner in which I was used) to get away from him as soon as possible. He would never allow me to leave the yard, unless it was for the purpose of taking out his horses to exercise them. At such times, I would often go to the fortune-teller, and by paying her twenty-five cents, she would tell me what she said my fortune would be. She told me I should eventually get away, but that it would be attended with a great deal of trouble; and truly, I experienced a vast deal of trouble before I could get away.

I will state to my readers some facts relative to the treatment I received from him, and others, during the time I lived there. He had an old black female slave whom he called Frankee. I always believed her to be a witch: circumstances to prove this, I shall hereafter state. He also had, at one time, a number of carpenters at work in his yard. One of them was a man about my size, and resembling me very much in dress, being dressed in a blue roundabout jacket. He came into the yard to his work one morning, with an umbrella in his hand. This old woman saw him come in, and thinking it was me, or pretending so to do, was the cause of my receiving a severe whipping, in the following manner. My master having mislaid his umbrella, had been looking for it for some time, and on inquiring of her about it, she told him that she saw me come into the yard with it in my hand. I was then in the yard; he called to me, and said, where have you been, sir? I replied, only to work about the yard, sir. He then asked me where I was all night with his umbrella? I told him I had not been out of the yard, nor had I seen his umbrella. He said I was a liar, and that I had taken his umbrella away, and was seen to return with it in my hand this morning when coming into the yard. I told him it was not so, and that I knew nothing about it. He immediately fell foul of me with a large stick, and beat me most unmercifully, until I really thought he would kill me. I begged of him to desist as I was perfectly innocent. He not believing me, still continued to beat me, until his strength was entirely exhausted.

Some time after this, my mistress found his umbrella where she had placed it herself, having removed it from the place where he had left it, and gave it to him, saying, you have beat him for nothing—he was innocent of it. I was afterwards informed by another servant of the circumstance. I then went to my master, and told him that he had beaten me most unmercifully for a crime I was not guilty of, all through the insinuation of that old woman. He replied, "No, by Gad, I never hit you a blow amiss: if you did not deserve it now, you did some other time." I told him she must have been drunk or she would not have told him such a story. He said that could not be, as she never was allowed to have any liquor by her. I told him to look in her chest, and convince himself. He then inquired of her if she had any rum. She said, no, sir, I have not a drop. I then told him that if he would look in her chest he would find it. He accordingly went, and found it. He then said to her, hey, you old bitch, I have caught you in a lie.

On this same account she [Frankee] appeared to be determined to kill me, by some means or other. I slept in the same room with her, under the kitchen. My blankets were on the floor. She had a straw bed on a bedstead about four paces from mine. My master slept directly over my head. I have heretofore stated that I was convinced that this creature was a witch, and would turn herself into almost any different shape she chose. I have at different times of the night felt a singular sensation, such as people generally call the night-mare. I would feel her coming towards me, and endeavoring to make a noise, which I could do quite plainly at first; but the nearer she approached me the more faintly I would cry out. I called to her, aunt Frankee! aunt Frankee! as plain as I could, until she got upon me and began to exercise her enchantments on me. I was then entirely speechless, making a noise like one apparently choking or strangling. My master had often heard me make this noise in the night, and had called to me, to know what was the matter; but as long as she remained there I could not answer. She would then leave me and go to her own bed.

After my master had called to her a number, of times, Frankee! Frankee! what ails Theo? (a name I went by there, cutting short the name Theodore,) she answered, hag ride him, sair. He then called to me, telling me to go and sleep with her. I could then, after she had left me, speak myself, and also have use of my limbs. I got up and went to her bed, and tried to get under her coverlid[36]; but not find her. I found her bedclothes wet. I kept feeling for her, but could not find her. Her bed was tumbled from head to foot. I was then convinced she was a witch, and that she rode me. I then lay across the corner of her bed without any covering, because I thought she would not dare to ride me on her own bed, although she was a witch. I have often, at the time she started from her own bed, in some shape or other, felt a shock, and the nigher she advanced towards me, the more severe the shock would be.

The next morning my master asked me what was the matter of me last night? I told him that some old witch rode me and that old witch is no other than old Frankee. He cursed me, and called me a damned fool, and told me that if he heard any more of it, he would whip me. I then knew he did not believe in witchcraft. He said, why don't she ride me? I will give her a dollar. Ride me, you old hag, and I will give you a dollar. I told him she would not dare to ride him.

One morning after he had given me such a severe pounding concerning the umbrella, and I was determined not to stay with him long, but to get away from him as soon as possible, he ordered me to fetch up my horse and saddle him, and put the other horse to the chaise, in order to go out to Bonaventure.[37] I did so, and whilst I was gone I tried to invent some project, to make him believe me unwell. The next morning

36. A variant of coverlet, a bedspread.

37. One of the earliest plantations in Savannah. The land for Bonaventure was granted to John Mullryne, an English colonel, in the 1750s. He operated the plantation until 1850. The next owner, Capt. Peter Wiltberger, converted the land into a now-famous cemetery.

I pretended to be sick. He asked me what was the matter with me? I told him I had a pain in my side. He then said to Miss A——, go and weigh out a pound of salts for him. She did so. He then came to me with the salts in a cup, and said, do you see this, sir—do you see this? By Gad, you shall take every bit of this. He then mixed up a slight dose and gave it to me, which I took. He then sent for a doctor, who came and felt my pulse, and then said it would be well enough to put a blister plaister on my side. He accordingly went home, spread a very large plaister, and sent it over, which my master caused to be put on my side, which drew a large blister there. All this I bore without being sick or unwell, in the least.

There was a man who had been to him repeatedly to see if he would sell me. He always refused, saying, no, I did not buy him to sell; and I will be damned if I do sell him,—I bought him for my own use. I saw that he knew I was determined to get a new master, and, he was the more determined to keep me. At length I refused to eat any thing, at all. He would often ask me why I would not eat. I answered him that I could not, I was very weak and unwell. Still he invented every method he could to induce me to eat, often setting victuals by my bedside, &c.

At length, one day he wanted me to go and fetch a load of wood. He said, come, make haste and get your dinner ready, I want you to be a clever fellow, and eat your dinner, then to take the horse and cart, and go out and fetch in a load of wood. The dinner was soon ready: he cut off some meat and other victuals, and gave me before he eat himself, saying, here now, take this, be a clever fellow; eat it, and go and fetch a load of wood. I told him I did not want it. He says, take it, sir, and eat it. I replied, I thank you, sir, I don't want it. Got tam your soul, you don't want it; ha, you Got tam son of a bitch, you don't want it, do you? He then took up a chair and came towards me, threatening to kill me. His wife being afraid he would, called to him in order to prevent him, saying, do not kill him; do not strike him with that chair. He set it down and called to Frankee, fetch me a rope, Got dam you, fetch me a rope. I will bind him fast, send him to jail, and let him have Moses' law, (which is thirty-nine lashes on the naked back.)[38] She fetched the

---

38. The biblical punishment for a criminal who has violated one of the Mosaic laws (Deuteronomy 25: 2–3).

rope, and he bound me, and was on the point of having me taken to, jail when I, dreading the whipping I knew I should be obliged to take if I went there, finally consented to eat my victuals, and behave myself well. I then eat the victuals, which I relished exceedingly well. Then I went to the woods, and fetched home a load of wood.

After that I again refused to eat anything at all; but pretended to be sick all the time. I also told Frankee to tell my master that I was subject to such turns every spring, and I should not live through this. She told him, which frightened him very much, thinking he should lose me, (which would grieve him as much as it would to lose a fine horse of the same value.) He then again tried to make me eat by the same means, often leaving victuals by my bedside at night, or order Frankee to do it. He would then inquire of her if I had eaten anything yet. She replied, no, sir, I have not seen him eat anything since last Friday noon. I had his horse to water every day; and as I went out of, or across the yard, where I knew he would see me, I would pretend to be so weak that I could scarcely go. I would stagger along, to make him think that I should fall every moment.

He one time called his wife to the window, saying, Misses, Misses, by Gad, come here, do you see him? He is almost gone; by Gad, I shall lose him; see how he staggers. By Gad, he has not eat a mouthful now for these three weeks. I must lose him, by Gad; do you see that? I would, however, have it understood, that during all this time I did not go without victuals. I sometimes could steal a little provision; and after driving my master to his plantation, I could sometimes run into the potatoe house, where I could find a few of them, which I ate raw. At other times I could find a bone, not quite stripped clean, which, together with what I stole, made me a comfortable subsistence; or as much so as the slaves generally receive. I was determined not to eat anything in his sight, or to his knowledge, in order to make him think he must either sell me or lose me.

One morning he sent me to eat my breakfast. I told him I did not want any. He said, go along and get your breakfast. I went, and returned. When I came back, he asked me if I had eaten my breakfast? I told him, no, sir, I thank you, I did not wish for any. You did not, did you? Gad dam you; you are sick, are you? You may die and be damned, by Gad;— you may die and be damned;—your coffin shall not cost me a quarter of a dollar, by Gad;—you, shall be buried on your face, by Gad;—you may die and be damned.

Which of us is most likely to receive that part of this blessing which is to take effect in the next life, I will not say. However, being determined to change my situation if possible, I went to one Major Lewis, a free black man, and very cunning. I gave him money to go to my master and run me down, and endeavor to convince him that I was really sick, and should never be good for anything. In a few days from this, my master came down in the kitchen and says, boy get up; there, boy, (holding it out in his hand,) here is the very money I gave for you: I have got my money again, and you may go and be damned; and don't you never step into my house again; if you do, I will split your damned brains out.

I then went to my new master, Mr. Oliver Sturges,[39] who came from Fairfield, Connecticut. He bought me to drive his carriage. A new coachman's dress, which he gave me, would have felt much better, if it had not been for the large blister that had been drawn upon my side. However, I rode down by my old master's, and cracked my whip with as much pride, spirit and activity, as one of Uncle Sam's mail carriers, who drives four horses, on a general post road, drunk or sober. My old master happening to see me pass in this manner, was very much chagrined to think he had sold me under the impression that I was just ready to die. He called his wife to the window and complained to her that she had urged him to sell me, and swore and cursed outrageously.

I was now under my sixth master, Mr. Sturges, who bought me from the Jew. Mr. Sturges was a very kind master, but exceedingly severe when angry. He had a new negro, by the name of Cato, with whom I got a fighting, and bit off his nose, just as my master was going to sell him, which injured the sale of Cato very much. For this I had to beg very hard to escape being whipped. I went to the fortune tellers, who told me that my master said that if he should take me on with him to New York, I should be free; so I knew that I should not go with him.

39. A business partner in Burroughs and Sturges, a successful cotton and commission firm, Oliver Sturges owned a third interest in the steamship *Savannah*, which was the first vessel to cross the Atlantic Ocean under her own steam in 1819.

I had always been in the habit of praying, ever since I knew what it meant; and whenever I went to church, to drive the carriage, I used to stand upon the steps and listen to the preaching. About this time I began to realize that I was a sinner, and that hell would be my portion if I should die in my present situation; and afterwards while I was living with Dr. Collock,[40] and under the advice of the Rev. Mr. Collock[41], whose voice and preaching harrowed up my soul with awful apprehensions, I sought and obtained the hope of salvation. Blessed be God, I know the path to heaven. I have had sweet communion with the Lord; but alas! I have erred, and gone astray from holiness.

My conscience used sometimes to upbraid me with having done wrong, after I had run away from my master and arrived in Connecticut; and while I was living in Southington, Conn. (where I spent some time, as will afterwards be told,) I went up on a high mountain and prayed to the Lord to teach me my duty, that I might know whether or not I ought to go back to my master. Before I came down I felt satisfied, and it did seem to me that the Lord heard my prayers, when I was a poor, wretched slave, and delivered me out of the land of Egypt, and out of the house of bondage; and that it was His hand, and not my own artfulness and cunning, which had enabled me to escape: therefore, if we trust in God, we need have no fear of the greatest trials; and though my heart has been pierced with sufferings keen as death, and drank from the cup of slavery the bitterest dregs ever mingled in it, yet, under the consolations of religion, my fortitude never left me.

As Mr. Sturges was intending to remove to New York, he sold out all his property, and every thing he could wish to part with. He talked very strong of taking me on with him to New York; but after consideration altered his mind, and hired me out to a Mr. Wolhopter[42], a printer, in Savannah. I lived with Mr. Wolhopter all that summer, and drove his

40. Doctor Lemuel Kollock (1766–1823) was one of Savannah's foremost physicians.

41. Reverend Henry Kollock (1778–1819), cousin of Dr. Lemuel Kollock, was pastor of Independent Presbyterian Church in Savannah from 1806 to 1819.

42. Phillip David Woolhopter was the founder and editor of the *Columbia Museum*, a Federalist newspaper in Savannah. He later partnered with Gurdon Isaac Seymour to form the *Columbia Museum and Savannah Advertiser* from 1797 to 1802.

horses and carriages all about there, and out to White Bluff,[43] where
he had hired a seat for the summer, supposing it to be a healthy situation, which indeed it was; but we were tormented with mosquitoes and
such other insects as infest that country, (called by different names,)
to a great degree, so that we could hardly sleep at nights. We were
alternately at this place and at Savannah for the space of four or five
months. At the expiration of that time, Mr. Wolhopter removed back
to Savannah, with his family, and I accompanied them.

I will here mention that during the time I resided at White Bluff, at
the request of Mr. Wolhopter I often went a fishing, and the rays of the
sun beating down more severe there than where I had formerly lived,
it created an ague and fever, which reduced me so low that even my
attending physician, Dr. Collock. (who attended me strictly for about
four months,) despaired of my life; and often since that time being
borne down, under the afflictions that a slave often experiences—and
indeed too often—I have wished his predictions had proved true. But
after Dr. Collock perceived I was convalescent, and gaining my health
and strength rapidly, he inquired of me, that provided he should buy
me, if I would be contented to live with him, drive his horses and carriage, occasionally wait in the house and at the table, and do such other
business as is necessarily required in a family.

With but few remarks I endeavor to give my readers but a faint representation of the hard treatment, ill-usage and horrid abuse the poor
slave experiences while groaning under the yoke of bondage:——that
yoke which is not easy, nor the burden light; but being placed in that
situation, to repine is useless; we must submit to our fate, and bear up,
as well as we can, under the cruel treatment of our despotic tyrants.

After Dr. Collock made this proposition to me, I replied that I had
been sold from my parents in Virginia, and felt anxious to see them
again once more; but if he would buy me, I would serve him faithfully
and freely for the term of five years, provided that at the expiration of
that time he would grant me my freedom, to be specified in writing;

43. Located on the Vernon River, eight miles southeast of Savannah. After
the Civil War, White Bluff became the home of many ex-slaves from the plantations of St. Catherine's Island.

to which he consented, and promised to have it done, and give me the writing to keep; but he never fulfilled his promise. He, however, wrote to Mr. Sturges, in New York, and told me that he had received a letter from him, in which he consented I should go and live with him, and directed me to leave Mr. Wolhopter's house and come to his place of residence, which I accordingly did; being then very low in health, not having recovered from the ague and fever, but after living with him for some time I recovered my health so far as to be able to perform my duty.

When I first went there, on account of my being unwell my mistress [Mrs. Kollock] did not like to have me sleep in the house, and so gave me a room up over the carriage house to sleep in. In this room there was a bedstead or bunk, made of boards. I understood, by some of the servants, that a man lately died there in a fit. In the course of the day I laid myself down on the bedstead with a blanket to rest, not being able to be about, as a very little exercise overcame me. After lying there about an hour, I was looking very steady up towards the roof of the building, when to my great horror and surprise I could plainly perceive a large bright, sparkling pair of eyes intently fixed on me, staring me full in the face. It instantly occurred to me that the bedstead I was then lying on belonged to the man who had died there, and that I (not having any liberty to use it) was doing wrong, and that this was a token for me to leave it. I accordingly took my blanket, spread it on the floor, and slept on that.

Presently after the cook, Jane, came up to fetch me something to eat, she inquired of me why I left the bedstead and lay on the floor. I replied to her that I was afraid I had done wrong in lying on it as long as I already had done, for I had received no liberty from any person so to do, and I was convinced in my own mind that the bedstead placed there belonged to the man who had died there; and that I thought I had seen a token for me to leave it, which I accordingly had done. I then told her the circumstances of the eyes and of my conjectures at the time, that I had no business there. She replied to me, sleep on it if you please, you are perfectly welcome to the use of it. My mistress not knowing any thing of what had happened, sent me word that I might have a lamp there to keep burning through the night. She then was very kind to me and used me well; but I could not endure the thoughts of sleeping there, and as soon as bed-time came, I took my blanket and went into the house, and slept in the parlor with the two boys who were then waiting in the house, named Sandy and Cyrus, (commonly called Cy.) This being all unknown to my mistress at that time, but she afterwards consented to have me sleep in the house, which I did during the time I lived there.

My readers, or many of them who are not credulous, will very likely be apt to disbelieve the assertion already made, but I can assure them that the whole is true. Where is the person who would be made easily to believe a story of this kind, unless he positively did know it to be a fact, and the circumstances can be attested to even now. Although they did not see what I did, there were some of them acquainted with the circumstances. This cook, who brought me my victuals, told me the place was said to be haunted. She had her information from the other servants, who also told me the same; also, that strange noises were heard, which had been heard by other persons who were sick and put up there by my master's orders to be taken care of; many of them had been removed on the same account, as they told that they were positive of hearing strange noises, and also seeing frightful sights. These stories, combined with what I myself saw, warranted me in my opinion to make this assertion. I think the house, without any doubt, is what people in general would call haunted. My readers may put their own constructions and draw inferences, I can barely state that I tell the truth.

This circumstance happened in the winter. The next summer my master, Dr. Collock, ordered me to get the horses and carriage ready, to take all the family off to Darien,[44] which I accordingly did. They went from thence to Cumberland Island,[45] and I returned to Savannah with the horses and carriage, alone. My master gave me a piece of bacon, or shoulder, smoked, which I suppose would weigh about six or eight pounds, which was the whole he left me to last all summer. He also left

44. Located on the Georgian coast, in McIntosh County, between Savannah and St. Mary's River. The town had been noted for its abundant production of cotton, rice, and indigo until a fire in 1813 and a hurricane in 1814 devastated the area's plantations.

45. A small barrier island located off southeastern Georgia.

a tierce[46] of rice to be divided among us about the house, in all eight or ten of us. After the rice was gone, we were allowed to each of us eight quarts of Indian corn per week; this was all we had to subsist on during his absence, which was about six or seven months. I also had a great deal to do about the house, and out on the plantation I had as much mowing as I could attend to.

At another time, when I was at work out in the country, at my master's country seat, I had slipped the head stalls or bridles over the horses heads in order to let them eat while they were harnessed to a wagon, as I had been using them to draw hay. I left them to eat while I went to eat my dinner. In the meantime, two or three small negro children got into the wagon and frightened the horses, so that they ran round the house in the yard a number of times; and in so doing, they dragged the wagon over, or so nigh a young tree which my master set great store by, that it was torn up or broken down. When my master returned from Cumberland Island, he inquired of the driver (Old Ben) what had become of the tree. Old Ben replied, the torm broke him down, massa; and my master knew no more afterwards about it. The wagon, that was also badly broken, we mended up as well as we could among ourselves: the harness, which being considerably injured, I carried to Mr. Kitchen, who being used to make and repair harnesses for my master, fixed it so that he (my master) never found that it had been broken or injured. All of this passed unnoticed by my master.

At the time Dr. Collock left Savannah, he left in his office an old man called Dr. Sherman to take charge of his office, and attend on such persons as should request his attendance, when he was gone. There were also, at the same time, two young gentlemen in the office, studying with my master; one of them named James M'Call, and the other, a young man, I think they called Mr. Ginneylack. He at different times had insulted these young gentlemen to such a degree, that they left the office. A short time after this he found a large paper containing a number of images drawn out with a pencil; one representing himself and others representing ducks, with their bills open, apparently in the attitude of squalling. On the paper was written something like this:—how

---

46. A cask containing approximately thirty-five gallons of provisions.

"How do you do, my good old friend?—how do you do?—how are your sore legs? We know that ducks quack, and Sherman is a quack," &c. It was supposed that he was a quack in the greatest degree. Dr. Collock was considered one of the best physicians in Savannah; but as he was obliged to go to Cumberland Island, and could get no other person of any repute to remain in his office and take charge of his business readily, and this old man (or doctor) being an indigent person, he, out of charity, let him remain in his office until his return, and transact such business in his line as the people should see fit to set him about.

The old man [Dr. Sherman], not knowing to whom to ascribe the (what he termed) libel, vented his malice on me, by asserting that I was the author of it, of which I was perfectly innocent; but he made my master believe it. He wrote to him while he was at Cumberland Island, and persuaded him that I was actually the author. At the time my master wished to return to Savannah, he wrote to his brother-in-law, Edward Campbell,[47] Esq., attorney-at-law, requesting him to come with me, with the carriage and horses, to Darien, in order to take him and his family home. We accordingly went on one day, met them there, and returned the next. After our return, my master took me into his office, and inquired of me about these images. I told him I knew nothing about it. He was very inquisitive about it, but I still told him I knew nothing about it; but as Sherman made him believe that I had done all this mischief, of course my mistress also believed it; and after that I could never please them, let me try my best endeavors, they still appeared to be dissatisfied.

I was one evening ordered to take my mistress and her sisters to Mr. Andrews'. I accordingly harnessed the horses, put them to the carriage, and drove (with the ladies) to the house where I was directed. They went in the house and stayed, I do not know how long. I stayed with the horses and carriage at the door, in order to take care of them. I waited for them until I fell asleep and was dreaming. When they came out of the house, they awoke me by their talking and laughing at the door. I did not know where I was, where I had been, nor where I was

47. Edward Fenwick Campbell was the brother of Maria Campbell (wife of Dr. Lemuel Kollock).

a going. I knew no more where I was than if I had been blindfolded. But I was afraid to let them know that I had been asleep, so I drove on directly towards the market, looking on the right hand and on the left, to see if I could recognize some house that I had before been acquainted with; but finding none I drove on. My mistress observing this, enquired of me why I did not take that route home, but I made her no reply, then turned towards the bay, thinking I was driving towards the commons. I then saw Mrs. Telfure's[48] house, and then I knew where I was. I then drove down to Judge Jones', and left her sisters[49] there, and continued on home with my mistress to Broad street. I do not think that my mistress, or either of the ladies ever suspected the reason why I took such a roundabout road to get home; but it was owing entirely to my falling asleep in the carriage while waiting at the door, and on awaking not knowing where I was.

At another time I was severely attacked with a toothache. My master drew one of my teeth, which fractured my jaw, and made it ache worse. He had often given me a great many bottles to clean and scour, and at this time gave me a great number. I went down under the bluff to get some sand for the purpose of cleaning them. While I was there I kept drinking spirits (in order to ease my jaw where the tooth was drawn,) till I got completely intoxicated, and did not return until nearly evening. *I was then a praying soul.* As I was returning back to my master's house, I called in at the Rev. Henry Collock's study or office. He seeing my condition, or the condition I then was in, immediately offered to attend prayers with me, which he did; we prayed there nearly half an hour. I went into his office with tears rolling down my bosom, and the floor of his office will be a witness to my tears until the day of judgment.

After our prayers were ended I came out, and the next time I saw him [Rev. Kollock], was within the walls of a cold prison; he came to the diamond hole,[50] and spoke to me, and asked me how I did, (I was at

48. Edward Telfare, a loyalist in the American Revolution, was the governor of Georgia in 1786 and again from 1790 to 1793.
49. Harriett T. Campbell and Mrs. Noble Wimberly Jones.
50. A round hole made by a diamond saw.

the time lying down on my blanket on the floor.) I answered him, I had a very bad jaw-ache. I then asked him to give me a book containing the Psalms of David, such an one as I was then reading. The next day he sent me a Bible. I, however, at the time I left this Parson Collock at his office went directly home to my master, who was his cousin. One was a worldly man, the other was a Christian.

Immediately after I went into the yard, my master had information of it, and then took me in his office; he asked me where I had been? I told him I had been after gravel to clean his bottles, and on account of the pain in my jaw, I had drank spirits until I was so much intoxicated that I dare not come back until then. He then, after having a long conversation with me, ordered me to go up stairs and lie down. I did so, but after I had lain there a few minutes, he came up, took me by the collar and ordered me to go into a room where he wanted to lock me up. At this time I suspected his intention of wishing to lock me up, in order that as soon as night came, he could send me to jail. I then pretended to be much more intoxicated than I really was, in hopes by that means to induce him to let me remain where I then was until morning; but he would not, and after a severe struggle, he effected the purpose he intended, and I was locked up in a room in the third story, or in the garret.

After sitting sometime I began to consider my situation. I observed a bedstead with a cord in it, which I concluded best for me to take out and let myself down from the window, and clear myself for the woods; but upon examination, I found the window so high from the ground, (after I had taken the cord from the bedstead,) that I feared to attempt the leap; I threw back the cord with despair, and then determined to force the door; it was in me a desperate undertaking, but I finally effected it. After coming down the stairs as still and shy as possible, that creature, Jane the cook, perceived me and gave the alarm. Immediately the cry of stop thief! stop thief! re-echoed from every quarter. I ran and they pursued, caught me, and brought me back. I was then bound and pinioned, my hands were closely tied behind, and I was conducted in this manner (in a more shameful manner than one half the prisoners, malefactors, or highway robbers, after having the sentence of death pronounced upon them, are taken to the place of execution) to jail.

There I staid eight long weeks, and what do you think my diet was during that time? Why, I will tell you, my reader, our allowance was to each person one quart of corn, ground and the husks fanned out of it, and then boiled, which we sometimes are allowed salt for, and at other times we are not. Oftentimes we were obliged to eat it without even salt or any other seasoning. As for meat, we are entirely a stranger to it, we know nothing about it, as an allowance either from our masters or the jailor. Our jailor having considerable to be done in and about the house, and knowing me to be expert in what he wanted to have done, released me from solitary confinement, and let me work for him about the prison at his own discretion; but one day Dr. Collock saw me out of jail on my ordinary business, while he was passing by, and came in and told Captain M'Call the jailor, that I would run away if he gave me such liberties. Mr. Griffin, then clerk of the jail, came and called to me and said, Grimes, your master says you will run away, and that you must be shut up again, for he does not like to see you out here. I was then conducted back to the cell again, where I remained until he again returned to Savannah; then I was restored as it were to liberty again, that is, to do what was necessary in and about the house; but I being a barber, fared rather better than the other prisoners.

I will state that I have seen women brought there and tied hand and foot, and their clothes turned up and tied there, up to their shoulders, leaving their bodies perfectly naked, then whipped with a keen rawhide (or cowskin sometimes called) until the blood ran down to their heels. I was then in expectation that my turn would be next, every moment looking for it. While I was in confinement, I myself, as well as the other prisoners, were used to the sound of Oh pray! Oh pray! which came from those poor slaves, then in preparation for being whipped, or experiencing then at the same time, the smart of the lash, which was so often used without mercy. As large, stout and athletic a negro as I was ever acquainted with, was selected for the purpose of whipping those who were doomed to receive the lash. He himself being there confined for some crime he had committed. In a case of whipping, he was compelled to put it on as severely as lay in his power, or take a severe flogging himself.

One man who was confined in the same room with me, by the name of Reuben, belonged to John Bolton, (one of the richest men in Savannah). This poor man's back was cut up with the lash, until I could compare it to nothing but a field lately ploughed. He was whipped three times in one week, forty stripes, save one, and well put on by this athletic fellow. You may well think this poor negro's back was not only well lacerated, but brutally and inhumanly bruised.

I at this time was in such dread of the whipping post, where I daily saw so many human beings sacrificed to the lash of the tyrant, that it struck me with horror. I prayed constantly to my God (who had relieved me before in the hour of danger,) to protect and defend me in this adversity, being now in a prison, from whence I knew no means of escape. And early one morning, while pondering on the miseries I was compelled to endure, I thought, and indeed was convinced, that I heard a voice from heaven, saying, Be of good cheer; and other words, which I do not conceive necessary to mention in this history. At the same time I heard this, I had a glimpse of something most glorious to behold. I immediately felt a comfort in my soul, which cheered me up, and made me feel joyful. I was then convinced that my prayers had ascended to the high throne of Grace, for which I returned my most fervent thanks to the Almighty Ruler of the Universe.

After remaining some time in jail, Dr. Collock came and took me out, and said his reason for keeping me there so long was, that he had expected a ship from New Orleans, and intended to send me there to work on the sugar plantation; but as the ship did not arrive, and he having considerable mowing to do on his plantation, he would take me out and set me at work to do his mowing, the other slaves not understanding it. So, after remaining in my solitary cell for eight long weeks, I was then permitted to breathe the fresh air again, and put to my task in the meadows, where I continued during that season, cutting and curing his grass. The winter following, I was employed in clearing and grubbing new ground.

The next summer I was kept on the plantation as usual, under the negro driver. When the season came for cutting oats, I was one day sent to mow them. I mowed one forenoon, and having a severe boil under each arm, did not feel able, nor indeed was I able to rake them up. I went to the room where I slept, it being out from Savannah about two or three miles, in a large house, where the driver and his family slept, I there laid down to rest myself. After about half an hour, the old negro driver came to me, and asked me why I did not rake up my oats, or those I had cut. I replied that I had a large boil under each arm, and was unable to do it. He swore I should do it, and went for a stick to beat me, in order to compel me to do it. I heard him coming back, and when he burst open the door, I let him have it in old Virginia style, (which generally consists in gouging, biting and butting.) I drove my head against him, (hardly knowing what I was about, being so much terrified) until he could scarcely stand or go.

I then compelled him to give up the stick to me, which I kept in my hand, walking to and fro, while he as soon as he recovered from the bruising I had given him, called aloud to the other slaves to come to his assistance. They immediately gathered together, to the number of about twenty. He ordered them to seize me, and was in hopes they would; but one of the stoutest of them, on whom he placed the greatest reliance, came up to me to enquire what was the matter, and why I had treated the driver so. I asked how I had treated him. He replied, how did you. I then seized him by the shoulders, and said to him, I will show you. So I served him in the same way I had the driver, and almost as severe. The other negroes seeing me use this stout fellow so harshly, were afraid to touch me. I kept walking with the stick I had taken from my enemy, to and fro as before. They did not attempt after that to touch me.

The driver then called to one of the slaves, to get a horse, and go to town, to give my master information; saying, Robert, Robert, gitta up a horse, and go uppa town tella massa Pero a whippa me. But they not attempting to meddle with me any more, I went myself to town, to see my master first. I arrived there after Robert had been there a short time. I went into my master's office and told him the whole affair. He enquired of me very particularly concerning it. I convinced him of my innocence, and he sent me back to the plantation again, to work as before.

During the conversation I had with my master, he asked me how I dare strike the driver, I replied that I must defend myself. He said to me, would you dare to strike me if I was out there? I answered, yes sir, I know my arm would be cut off if I should attempt to strike you; but sir, if you had been there you would not have used me in the way the driver did; he is an ignorant old African, or Guinea negro, and has not judgment sufficient to superintend any one in my present situation. I then showed him my boils. He was satisfied I was not able to rake the oats, but said, when I leave my driver there, I put him in my shoes; go back to the plantation, I shall be there soon myself. I told him I had no friend, except it was himself, and if he did not whip me when he came to the plantation, I should be convinced he was my friend; and furthermore I was convinced that not one negro on the plantation was friendly to me. He knew me to be a stranger, and a man of good sense. After this conversation, I went back to the plantation, and staid there until he came.

When he arrived there, he called the old driver, and talked to him very severely, saying, you should have examined into his situation before you undertook to whip him; you would then have been satisfied he was not able to work. He said not three words to me in anger. I continued to work on the plantation until towards winter, when I was again sent to the woods, and employed in cutting and splitting rails.

I should have mentioned, that while working on the plantation the summer past, I undertook to raise for myself a small crop of rice, of perhaps twenty rods of ground. It being the first I had ever undertook to raise, it cost me considerable trouble. All that I knew about it, was what little information I could get from seeing the negroes raise here and there a small piece for themselves; and I was obliged to do it in the same way; that is, to take an opportunity occasionally, when not being observed by the driver, to slip in and do a little at it. After it was in a situation to cut I reaped it and carried it to town, where I sold it for $1.25 per hundred, amounting in the whole to about $5 or $6. I kept this money, that in case of emergency, I could occasionally purchase a small piece of meat, or other necessary articles, for my subsistence. I sometimes went to town in order to procure something to eat with our common allowance, (a peck of corn per week) and have often carried on my head a bundle of wood, perhaps three miles, weighing more than one hundred pounds, which I would sell for twelve cents, in order to get a supply of necessary food. I would then, it being late in the evening, go to my master's house unknown to him, and lodge there.

It has frequently been the case, that I have been so much fatigued with my day's work, and then carrying my bundle of wood that distance, that I have overslept myself, or slept longer than I intended. In that case, I have been obliged to get out at the window, or in some other way avoid my master, who used to visit his plantation early each morning, so that I could get there first. I would then, after running three miles, start the negroes out to work, telling them my master was coming. They would all go out at once, and by the time he arrived, be steadily engaged at their work. Thus I gained for my master a great many hours work in the course of the season, which he knew nothing about, and all for the purpose of clearing myself from blame, and perhaps a severe flogging.

By this manner, I was enabled to acquire a very comfortable subsistence through the winter, or during the time I lived with Dr. Collock. He sold me some time in the winter. To do the Doctor justice, I must say that he was the best and most humane man I ever lived with, or worked under.

Some time previous to my master's selling me I had heard that A. S. Bullock, Esq. agent for the navy,[51] (who had engaged a carriage and pair of horses, coming on from New York, which he expected very soon,) wanted to buy a servant, to drive and take care of them. I went to see him, and enquired if he would buy me. He replied yes, if your master will sell you. I then went to my master and told him Mr. Bullock wished to buy me, provided he would sell me. He then said to me, where did you see Mr. Bullock? have you been there to try to induce him to buy you? I replied, no sir, he saw me in the street and enquired of me whether my master wished to sell me. I told him you did. He then said go and tell your master I will buy you if he will sell you; he then asked me what price my master would require for me, I told him $500 was the price for which I was last sold; he replied I will give that sum for you if Dr. Collock will accept of it. He added tell your master if he wants to sell you, that I wish him to come and see me. My master replied, if Mr. Bullock wants to see me, let him come here, I shall not go to see him. I then went and told Mr. Bullock the answer my master gave me; he asked me if my master would give me a recommend. I answered him that he said he would give me none. He then observed to me, I perceive your master does not want to sell you. He then called his little son to him (aged about twelve years) and gave him between

---

51. Archibald Stobo Bulloch was a Savannah alderman (1812–14) and the son of Archibald Bulloch (1730–77), Georgia's first state president.

five and six hundred dollars, telling him to go to Dr. Collock, give him the money and tell him if he was willing to sell Grimes, to take that and send back as much change as he pleased. He took $500, and sent back the remainder.

I was now sold to Mr. Bullock, where I stayed without returning to see my old master. I felt very uneasy whilst the boy was gone, fearing my master would not sell me, as I was satisfied his intention was not to sell me in Savannah, but to send me off to New Orleans, or some other place at a distance, being as I was convinced in my own mind, so much prejudiced against me by that old quack (so called) *Sherman*, that he was determined if he sold me at all, that it should not be in Savannah. It is generally known that when a man sells a servant, he intends by that means to punish him, and endeavors to sell him where he shall never see him again. For this same reason I was afraid Dr. Collock would not sell me, my mistress also being opposed to my being sold in Savannah.

I shall here mention a very narrow escape I had while I lived with Dr. Collock. As I was occasionally tending his horses and driving them, I was exposed very often to be hurt by them, to be killed, bit, thrown off them &c. He had one very ill-natured cross horse, no one could approach him or pass behind him with any safety. I was one day compelled to go in great haste in the reach of him. As I got almost past him, he threw both his feet against me with such violence, that my breath was entirely beat out of my body, and I was completely stunned; he sent me at a distance where I lay completely senseless for some time; I barely escaped with my life. After some time I got up, went and informed my master and mistress of the circumstances, when the necessary remedy was administered, and I finally recovered. This I mention, merely to inform my readers of the dangers and narrow escapes I have experienced during my slavery.

The same parson Collock, whom I have heretofore mentioned, was a very fine candid and humane man; he was beloved by every one who was acquainted with him; a friend to the poor slave, as well as the richest planter, or gentleman, he was in a habit of holding meetings in the evening, as often as two or three times each week, which I always attended to strictly, and very often it was as late as 10 o'clock, or later, before I reached my master's house. He had a number of times on finding me not at home in the evening, enquired of the other servants where I was, and was generally by them told that they did not know unless I was at meeting; he one evening after my return, appeared to be very angry with me, and asked me where I had been so late for a number of evenings. I replied, I have been to meeting, sir. He then said by what means do you escape the vigilance of the guard?[52] (or what they term in the northern states *watch*.) I replied the guard do not meddle with me in returning from meeting. He then said, why do they not? they ought to. I said nothing to this, but I knew very well what he wished, that was, he would be very well pleased to have the guard take me up, and take me to jail, in order to punish me for attending meeting; but the guard never attempted to meddle with me—they always took me to be a *white man*.

I have frequently walked the streets of Savannah in an evening, and being pretty well dressed, (generally having on a good decent suit of clothes,) and having a light complexion, (being at least three parts white,) on meeting the guard, I would walk as bold as I knew how, and as much like a gentleman; they would always give me the wall. One time in particular, while walking home late in the evening I saw two or three of them together. I was afraid, but summoned all my resolution; and marched directly on towards them, not turning to the right hand nor the left, until I came up to them. They at first did not notice me, being engaged in conversation. I continued on, head up, walked past them and happening to brush one of them a little in passing, they immediately turned off the walk; one of them spoke and said we ask your pardon sir.

At another time I deceived them in the following manner: One evening a colored man from Richmond, Virginia, called on me while sitting in the kitchen, and told me he had lately been waiting on my old master, Doct. Philip Thornton, of Richmond, and had taken him from there to his father's country-seat, at Monpelier, in Culpepper County, in a carriage with four horses, but was at present waiting on a gentleman from Richmond, then in town, who lodged at Col. Shelman's tavern,

52. In 1770, the Georgia legislature created the "Savannah Watch" an appointed group of white male citizens responsible for patrolling city streets in an effort to prevent slave escapes and revolts.

some distance from my master's. He told me his name was William Patterson, he was a free man, and was hired by people occasionally to drive their horses. He had heard of me while at Doct. Thornton's, and by enquiring of Major Lewis, a black man, who was a great groom in Savannah, he found where I lived. He stayed with me, taking something to drink, and smoked a cigar (my master knowing nothing of it) until about eleven o'clock, when he wanted to return to his lodgings. I told him the guard were all out at their posts, and it would be dangerous for him to attempt it alone; but if he would consent to walk behind me in the capacity of a servant, (to all appearances,) I would accompany him home, and I had no doubt but I could deceive the watch as I had done before. He readily consented to this, and I put on my best suit, took a rattan[53] in my hand, he walked behind me and continued on until we reached the tavern, where we found about fifteen or twenty of the guard seated on the steps of the door; he trembled, but I walked directly on, when they rose up to make room for me to enter and him to follow. I opened the door and went in, he closed it. After he had followed me as a servant through the streets, and made the watch believe it, when we were alone by ourselves, he flourished his hands, and snapped his fingers a great number of times, saying, well done, well done for you; I will tell this when I get home to Virginia; I should not dared to have undertaken so desperate a thing.

During the time I lived with A. S. Bullock, Esq., the navy agent, at first he treated me very well. After living with him about a fortnight, the horses and carriage he had expected arrived. The horses were very low in flesh. I took them into my care, attended them strictly, and they soon began to thrive: in about three or four weeks they were in good order. By this time my master knew, or at least thought, I understood the business of taking care of horses, and was very well pleased with my performance, as I kept the carriage, horses and harness very clean and nice. During the winter and summer after, I used to drive the horses and carriage, carrying some part or the whole of his family out for a ride every evening, about five o'clock. The distance was generally from

53. A walking stick or cane made from the stem of various climbing palm plants.

three to five miles. The winter following I was employed generally as during the one past. The next spring he sold his horses and carriage to Doct. Jones, who was an enemy to me, and exerted all the arts he could invent, to influence my master against me; but all availed nothing, my master being well pleased with me and I with him, he could not effect his purpose.

At this time my mistress,[54] her sister, Mrs. Hunter, with her daughter, Miss Catherine, and a brother of my mistress, Mr. Glen, took passage in a packet, with a great number besides, for New York. My master concluded to go by land, and to buy a light carriage, with a pair of horses; one Mr. Lyon to join with him, and for me to go and drive the horses. After having everything almost completed for the journey, they altered their minds, and concluded to take passage in the stage. If I had gone on with Mr. Bullock to the northward, I should have returned, had it been, for no other purpose than to make out my enemies to be liars, who had instilled into my master a belief that if he took me with him I would never return, but run away and leave him.

I was then left, by my master's order, to work out and pay him three dollars per week, and find myself. I then went to work for Mr. Irving, on board the Epervier,[55] who was manager on board. He gave me one dollar for each day I worked there. The Epervier was a vessel taken from the British in the last war. I saw seven truck loads of gold and silver, in boxes, taken from her and carried to the bank in Savannah. I worked for Mr. Irving about a month, he paid me off, and I worked about town for a few days after. I then went out on a plantation and worked for a Mr. Houston. He also gave a dollar a day. I worked for him about a week at mowing. After that I came back and went to work on board the James Monroe, a national vessel,[56] for Capt. Skinner, of New London,

54. Probably Mrs. Archibald Stobo Bulloch (Mary DeVaux), daughter of John and Sarah Jones Glenn.

55. A British man-of-war captured and brought into the Savannah port by the American sloop-of-war the *Peacock* in May 1814.

56. The *James Monroe* was not a U.S. Navy vessel. It was commissioned as a privateer in the War of 1812. As late as the spring of 1815, Captain Skinner's ship was still actively seizing prizes off the coast of France and Spain, unaware

Connecticut. He gave me seventy-five cents a day. I acted as cook and steward on board of her. After this I went to work about town, and Mr. Burrows,[57] a brother-in-law of my master, hired me to drive his horses and carriage. He gave me twenty dollars a month. I carried him and his family to Augusta. I resided with him all that summer, and drove his horses and carriage from there, up the same hills, back and forth, each day, when the weather was good, for about six months, which was as long as my master would spare me. Mr. Stephen Bullock, a relative of my master, (as he was left superintendent of his affairs during the time he was absent,) wrote to Mr. Burrows that he must send me home. Accordingly I went back on horseback.

A few weeks after my return, my master and family arrived from New York, with a carriage and four elegant horses. I now had six horses to take care of, and the carriage to keep clean and in order. I took such good care of the horses, and kept the carriage so nice, that Mr. Bullock was well pleased with me. After I had got the four new horses in good order, and fat, he sold one pair of them, which relieved me from some trouble and labor. We have never had any disagreement, yet he had been on to the northward, and but just returned.

Some time after this my master bottled up a few dozen of wine, counted them and delivered them into my care for keeping. At this time he had a number of workmen, joiners[58] and carpenters at work about the house. When I took the wine into my care, I took it out of the cellar, and as I was gone after a basket, one of the workmen took a bottle and secreted it. My object in going after a basket was to carry it up into the garret, and this man passing that way, took that opportunity to steal a bottle of it, perhaps not considering at the same time that I was

---

of the truce ending the war. Later that spring and summer of 1815, Captain Skinner took the *James Monroe* on two training voyages in Nova Scotia. Grimes may have met Captain Skinner on the *James Monroe* sometime after September 1815; but more likely, he was aboard the ship in 1814 when it visited the port of Savannah as a regular merchant vessel.

57. Benjamin Burroughs, business partner with Oliver Sturges (Grimes's sixth master).

58. A carpenter who specializes in constructing doors, cabinets, stairs, and other permanent woodwork.

responsible for it, and should be liable to receive a severe punishment if the bottles were not all found: but he did not even return the bottle after drinking the contents. After I carried them up stairs, my master went and counted them, and finding one missing, called to me to know where it was. I told him I had set them all out of the cellar, and then went for a basket to carry them up; and I had carried the whole that I found up garret. He said there was one missing, and ordered me to fetch it immediately. I told him I thought I had carried up the whole of them. We then went together and counted them a number of times, but found one missing. He was very angry with me. I asserted my innocence repeatedly, but all to no purpose. I could not make him believe me not guilty.

I was suspicious that some one of the mechanics had taken it. I went to them and enquired about it. One of them acknowledged that he had taken it, and was willing to pay my master for it. I then immediately went and informed my master, but he would not believe me. I returned to the man who took it, and requested him to go with me to my master, in order to convince him of my innocence. He consented, and we went together. He made a statement to him of the whole affair, and also told him he was willing to pay him to his full satisfaction. But whether my master had an idea that there was a connivance between us to clear myself, or what his motive was I cannot tell, but he did not appear to be any more satisfied than before; still telling me I took it.

It grieved me very much to be blamed when I was innocent. I knew I had been faithful to him; perfectly so. At this time I was quite serious, and used constantly to pray to my God. I would not lie nor steal. My master knew nothing of that. I kept it a profound secret from him. When I considered him accusing me of stealing, when I was so innocent, and had endeavored to make him satisfied by every means in my power, that I was so, but he still persisted in disbelieving me, I then said to myself, if this thing is done in a green tree what must be done in a dry?[59] I forgave my master in my own heart for all this, and prayed to God to forgive him and turn his heart. I was dissatisfied to think that

59. Luke 23:31: "For if they do these things in a green tree, what shall be done in the dry?"

my master had so bad an opinion of me at the time I was so honest; and tried by best endeavors to please him.

I then wanted some person to buy me, and let me work until I had paid $800. I accordingly applied to a man who promised me he would try to buy me. I must here state the circumstance that prevented him from doing so. Sometime previous to this, I had told the other servants that something would happen to me, that my master would be very angry with me for something, that he would beat me unmercifully and send me to prison. They were very much surprised to hear me talk in this manner as they well knew that we were on very good terms at that time. So after this happened concerning the wine, I having a number of articles in and about the yard, such as boxes, clothes, trunks, &c., and as I have before mentioned, being determined to get some person to buy me, I used occasionally to carry some of them off and hide them in the woods, well knowing that if my master should sell me, he would never allow me to enter his yard again; and the things being my own, would be of service to me in another place, should I be so fortunate as to have a new master.

After obtaining the promise of this man to buy me, he being unwilling to speak to him on the subject, fearing my master might think he was endeavoring to entice me away, he told me to ask my master if he wanted to sell me. I shall not mention the name of this man, for as it so happened he did not buy me, it might make some difficulty. Ever since the circumstance of the wine, my master not appearing to be satisfied with me about it, had treated me very severely. I determined one day when my master was in the parlor to ask him the question. So I went into the kitchen which was in the lower room where the other servants were, (having been myself in the stable attending to the horses,) and told them that what I had prophesied would soon take place, saying, my hour is come, I am now going up to see my master, and he will beat me and put me in prison. They then enquired of me what was the matter. I answered them that I was going to ask my master a question, for which I shall receive this. They endeavored to persuade me not to go, saying, you will only bring trouble on yourself by going. But being determined on doing it, I went, not heeding what they said, begging of me not to go.

I went up. He [Mr. Bulloch] was walking backwards and forwards (with his hands thrust in his pockets) across the room, waiting for his dinner. I stood for a few moments behind a chair, with my hand on the back of it, fearing to speak. At length he stepped up toward me, saying, well what's wanting, Grimes? I being so fearful to irritate him, dared not speak immediately. He repeated, well, Grimes, what's wanting? I then with a great deal of diffidence (after many fruitless attempts to speak) said, master, are you willing to sell me? It was exactly as I had anticipated; he flew into a violent passion, caught hold of a chair and came towards me in the attitude of attempting to strike me; he made one or two passes at me with it, but dropping it, seized me by the collar and beat me with his fist most unmercifully; at the same time exclaiming, sell you? yes, you damned son of a bitch. God damn you, I'll sell you; I'll sell you by God; who wants to buy you? God damn you, who wants to buy you? I made no reply, but cleared myself from him and his house as soon as possible for the stable.

While going towards the stable, not daring to turn my head, and expecting him every moment at my heels, I pretended to stop to pick up something, at the same time casting my eyes behind me, I saw him coming very rapidly towards me. I had hoped as his dinner was nigh ready, he would not undertake to come after me until after dinner, and had determined on quitting him immediately, thinking it best to go then, as I was convinced he would when he next saw me finish what he had begun, that is a severe beating; but seeing him so near, and pretending not to have seen him, I went into the stable, took my fork, and went to work stirring up the straw, not noticing him at all, or at least not letting him know that I did. He came into the stable and seized me by the collar with his left hand, while with his right fist clenched, he beat me with that in my breast and face, until all in a gore of blood. I dared not say a word, but pretended to be very much hurt; he all the time exclaiming, who wants to buy you? God damn you, I say, who wants to buy you, you rascal? He then dragged me to the platform under the Piazza,[60] continuing all the time to beat me in the same manner, but calling frequently to Jack to bring a rope and bind me. He said, bring me a rope, Jack, bring a rope, God damn you, and bind this rascal? Jack went for a rope, but not being able to find one as soon as he wanted, my

60. A colonnaded veranda.

master was quite enraged at him, and fell to beating him severely. After some time Jack found a rope and fetched it to my master, but he was so much enraged at me, that he kept beating him, saying, tie him, you rascal, tie him sir. All that poor Jack could do was to smart under his chastisement, and keep saying, yes sir, yes sir, I will. I was then placed in such a situation that my arms were pinioned, and my hands tied behind.

He then sent Jack for a constable, saying, go, you rascal, and find a constable; have this damned rascal taken to jail. Jack went, but soon came back, saying, I could not find Master Nobie. He then told him to go and get any constable he could find. He soon came with another. My master told this constable to take me to jail, and give me a flogging, and lock me up. This man, seeing my situation—my face all blood, my hands bound behind me, and I standing there trembling with the bruises I had received, together with the fear of another more barbarous flogging, appeared to take pity on me. He whispered to my master and said, I think, by his looks, you have given him a severe whipping; I would put him in jail without any more chastisement. My master replied, by God, I have not hurt him; all I have done was with my knuckles. I had repeatedly told my master before that my hands were so closely bound the blood was almost ready to start through my fingers. He replied I don't care if it should. He then directed the constable (as he had persuaded him not to flog me any more) to take me to jail. We started and got as far as the gate, when he called him back, saying, let Jack wash the blood off his face; it has not been washed for six months, people will think I have been murdering him. He then told Jack to go and get my hat, and put it on me, and also my coat, and spread it over my shoulders, which he did. I then went with the constable to jail, and was locked in.

I knew my master's disposition so well that I was convinced he did not wish to have me imprisoned; but only for me to make an acknowledgment and ask his pardon, for merely my asking him the question I did. I had before anticipated this, for I knew he could not do without me: all he wanted of me, to set me at liberty, was for me to ask his pardon, and promise never to ask him to sell me again. Had he (at the time the constable advised him not to have me whipped again) persisted in having his orders executed, which I knew to be Moses law, that is, 40 stripes, save one, which I must receive before I entered the jail, I should have begged his pardon, and made almost any acknowledgment he should require, knowing my constitution could not bear it. But I pretended to be ignorant of the whole, and acted stupid and dull, not regarding what I knew to be his wish; and when I heard him order the constable to commit me without whipping, my heart leapt for joy, for I knew what I had to endure before I should be sold. After lying in jail some time, I sent word to this same man who had promised to buy me, to come and buy me out of jail; but he refused, thinking my master would conjecture he had enticed me to leave him, notwithstanding I had assured him that my master wished to sell me.

After that I was compelled to lie there in my solitary cell for the space of three weeks, before any person appeared to buy me. The room in which I was placed was so foul and full of vermin, it was almost insupportable. The lice were so thick and large that I was obliged to spread a blanket (which I had procured myself) on the floor, and as they crawled upon it, take a junk or porter bottle,[61] which I found in the jail, and roll it over the blanket repeatedly, and in the same way that I have seen people grind or powder mustard seed on a board. I could always hear the death of some announced by their cracking. This I had to observe daily, and indeed often two or three, and perhaps more times each day. Besides all this, I had often to take off my shirt, pick them out of my collar, pile them up as fast as I could, and take the bottle to crush them.

My readers will here understand that this room had constantly, previous to my imprisonment therein, been occupied as a prison for negroes. They, no more than myself having a privilege of a change of linen, or water wherewith to cleanse it. Any person would naturally suppose the place to be (vulgarly speaking) filled with lice; and it was, when I went there, as nigh filled as any building I ever entered.

I will here mention that a few days previous to the time that I told the servants something would take place between my master and myself dissatisfactory to us both, that for some trivial fault, which I cannot now recollect, he came to the stable, took the reins of the harness, bound my hands, and led me along the stables (the doors being open,) backwards and forwards, for some time, threatening to whip

61. A nineteenth-century glassmaker's term for a beer, cider, or porter bottle.

me. The windows in the house being open, my mistress saw him. She then went to the back door and called Ben (a servant) from the kitchen. He came to her. She immediately seized him by his ear, and, shaking him severely, pointing at the same time to me, (having a fair view and grinning horridly a ghastly smile,) said, you see there! you see there! Do you see how your master does with Grimes? he will do so with you, too. She then called Jack, a poor, honest Guinea negro, and a faithful servant, to her, and used him in the same way, saying, if you do not behave yourself well, you shall be served in the same manner. They replied, yes, mistress, I will! I will!

It was a practice of my master to have a soup almost every day. My master Stephen usually went to market each day to procure meat for dinner for the family, and always purchased a shin of beef. Jack accompanied him with the market basket to fetch home what he bought. The richest pan of the soup was consumed by the family, and the remainder, consisting of the lean meat, and the shin, and coarse pieces remaining on the bones, were then left for us in the kitchen. Gulla Jack, who was a servant about the house, to scour, &c., the same that fetched the meat home, after noticing this for a number of months, began to be dissatisfied with it. One day in particular we were standing together under the platform, back of the house, my master being in the necessary, but a few yards from us, heard his conversation, which amounted to nearly what I now am about to state. Jack said to me, (not knowing our master was so near,) be Gad, I don't want to stay here for my master to licka me, an licka me, an all he give me a sin of beef; he eata all de meat, and den he licka me wid de bone. Be Gad, me do not lika stay here to be usa so.

Using such kind of broken language as he had often before used to me, when I would laugh and join with him, merely for sport, and to hear him talk; at this time I joined with him and laughed heartily. After this I went to the stable to work, and Jack went to his work. My master went into the house and went up stairs, when he told my mistress what he had heard. Whilst he was telling her, one of the servant girls happened to overhear him. She came directly and informed Jack and myself of it, saying our master was quite angry with us for it. We were both very much frightened at this information, and knew not what to do. I had cleaned his shoes for him, and sent them up by the girl; he sent them back again, saying, they were not half cleaned. I did it again, and made them very nice, and sent them up again. He sent them back a second time, with orders for me to fetch them up myself. I was now more afraid than before, but I took them up to him in the parlor. When I went in he was very angry: he snatched up the poker and thrust it hastily into the fire with the greatest fury, exclaiming, what! you are above cleaning my shoes, are you? By God, you are above cleaning my shoes; you can carry on with Jack about a shin of beef, but you are above cleaning my shoes. I replied that I did not mean any harm by that, but only laughed to hear Jack use his broken language. He then said Jack was not to blame, but it was me altogether, for I knew better; but he was a poor, ignorant Guinea negro, and therefore not so much to blame.

My master would always, when the weather was bad, order me to drive the horse and chaise[62] to his office, and carry him home to dinner, precisely at two o'clock. One time I being detained longer than usual, did not arrive there until after the clock had struck. I met him about fifty yards from his office on his way home; I drove up to him in order to have him get in; but he took no notice of me at all, and continued on towards home; I drove a little forwards and turned about, overtook him, and asked him if he would ride. He looked at me very sternly and replied, no, I'll walk, as I began it. I then drove home and told Ben about it. He said to me, ah! you look out for that. I might mention a great many similar circumstances, but it would be too tedious a task, and I will leave it here.

After I had got through with all my trouble with Mr. Bullock, a Mr. White came and bought me out of jail for five hundred dollars. He came to the jail and spoke to me, saying he would buy me if I would consent to drive his horses. I told him I would. I was accordingly let out of jail soon after, and went to his house. I found him to be a cross, crabbed man. I did not stay with him long. I lived with him perhaps two or three months, when a certain Mr. Welman[63] came to my master's and bought me. This was the eighth time that I had been sold for five hundred dollars each time. My master did not buy me for his present use. He hired me out to Mr. Oliver Sturges, the man who had owned

---

62. A two-wheeled carriage drawn by a single horse.

63. Francis Harvey Welman (1780–1861), a Bermuda native, was a resident and merchant in Savannah.

me before. I worked for Mr. Sturges about four or five months. He had a man from New York, whom he hired for thirty dollars per month; he wanting to go home, Mr. Sturges offered Mr. Welman the same wages for me. Whilst I was there I drove his horses, took care of his carriage, and occasionally attended the people in the house.

I have experienced the sufferings of a slave in the Southern States. I have travelled from Frederickstown in Maryland, to Darien in Georgia and from there to Savannah, from whence I made my escape in the following manner. While I belonged to Mr. Welman he went with his family to Bermuda, and left me to work for what I could get, by paying him three dollars per week. During this time the brig Casket,[64] from Boston, arrived. I went with a number more to assist in loading her. I soon got acquainted with some of these Yankee sailors, and they appeared to be quite pleased with me. Her cargo chiefly consisted of cotton in bales. After filling her hold, they were obliged to lash a great number of bales on deck. The sailors, growing more and more attached to me, they proposed to me to leave, in the centre of the cotton bales on deck, a hole or place sufficiently large for me to stow away in, with my necessary provisions. Whether they then had any idea of my coming away with them or not, I cannot say; but this I can say safely, a place was left, and I occupied it during the passage, and by that means made my escape.

The evening before the brig was to sail I went with a colored man (a sailor on board) up into town and procured some bread, water, dried beef, and such other necessaries that I should naturally want. It was late in the evening, and he being a Yankee sailor, I directed him to walk behind me in the capacity of a servant, (as they would consider me his master, the watch or guard being all on their posts;) he did so, and we procured every thing necessary for me, took them on board, and I stowed them away in the hole left for me, where I myself went and remained until we arrived at the Quarantine Ground, New York.[65]

64. The *Casket* was built in Newbury, Massachusetts, and enrolled at port on April 22, 1815. It frequently traded in Savannah and, on each occasion, carried a cargo of cotton.

65. In 1760, the port of New York began enforcing quarantines on incoming vessels. In 1801, Tompkinsville, Staten Island became the formal quarantine location for ships and passengers coming into New York.

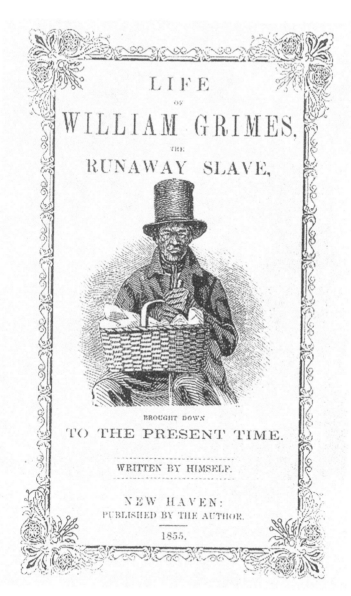

1. 1855 cover of *Life of William Grimes, the Runaway Slave.* (Courtesy of the New Haven Colony Historical Society)

2. Colonel William Fitzhugh (1651–1701) was the founder of Eagle's Nest, home to fourteen generations of the Fitzhugh-Grymes clan in King George County, Virginia. In his day, he was one the wealthiest men in Virginia. When he died at age fifty, he left his heirs over fifty-four thousand acres of land. He is Benjamin Grymes's third maternal grandfather. (Portrait courtesy of the Virginia Historical Society)

3. Portrait of the children of Philip Grymes (1721–62) and Mary (Randolph) Grymes of the Brandon estate, Middlesex County. They are first cousins of Benjamin Grymes, the father of William Grimes, the Runaway Slave. Like the Fitzhughs, the Grymeses owned several sizable plantations throughout Virginia. (Courtesy of the Virginia Historical Society)

4. A recently preserved Montpelier estate, home of Col. William Thornton, second owner of William Grimes, in Rappahannock County, Virginia. (Courtesy of Robert M. Thornton)

5a. Family Bible of the African American Grimes clan, marriages.
(Courtesy of R. E. Mason)

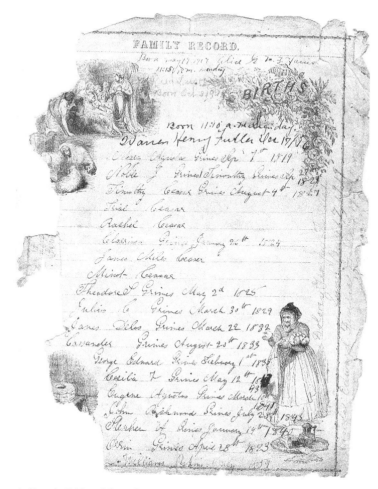

5b. Family Bible of the African American Grimes clan, births.
(Courtesy of R. E. Mason)

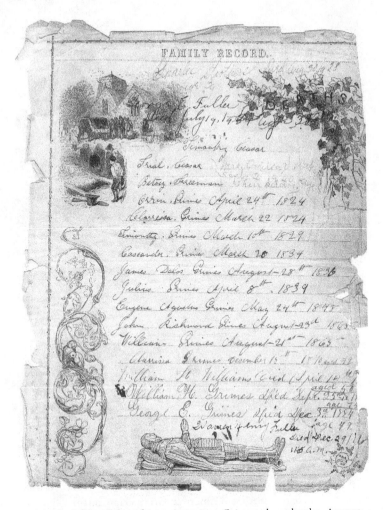

FAMILY RECORD.

DEATHS

Fuller
July 19, 1844 Aug 30

Timothy Ceasar
Seal, Ceasar
Betsy Freeman
Orrin Grimes April 24th 1824
Clarissa Grimes March 22 1824
Timothy Grimes March 10th 1829
Cassander Grimes March 20 1834
James Delos Grimes August 28th 1836
Julius Grimes April 8th 1839
Eugene Augustus Grimes May 24th 1843
John Richmond Grimes August 23d 1865
William Grimes August 21st 1865
Clarissa Grimes December 18th 18
William H Williams died April 14
aged
William H. Grimes died Sept 25
age 73
George E. Grimes died Dec 3d 1884
Nancy Henry Fuller
age 47
died Dec 29
1:15 a.m.

5c. Family Bible of the African American Grimes clan, deaths. August 21, 1865—the recorded death date of William Grimes as noted in the Grimes–Fuller family Bible. (Courtesy of R. E. Mason)

6–10. Preserved letters negotiating the freedom of William Grimes. The first letter is from Abel Catlin to Joseph Burrows (business partner of Oliver Sturgis, the sixth owner of William Grimes). Catlin offers to relinquish Grimes's home in exchange for the fugitive's freedom. The August 21, 1824, letter from the slave's final master—Francis H. Welman—informs H. T. Thompson, Esquire, to "execute proper and sufficient papers for the freedom of my fellow Theodore." Theodore was the name given to Grimes while he was enslaved in Savannah. (Courtesy of the Litchfield Historical Society)

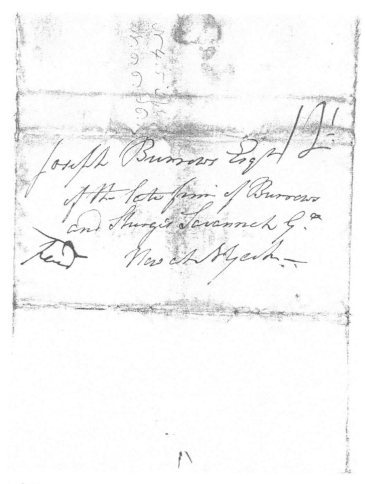

6a. Letter 1

Litchfield Co. Sept. 2d. 1822

Joseph Burrows Esquire

Sir, William Grimes, who lived several
years in this place called on me yesterday,
and stated the interview he had with you
in Albany, which drove forth the circumstance
of his leaving &c. — and the manner in which
he passed from Virginia &c. which was before
unknown, I believe in this place. At his request
I write you, and state, what he proposes to be
willing to do, and what, I believe he can, that
is, to surrender every thing in his power for
his freedom. He has property in this place
which I think may be worth 4 or 400 fifty
dollars, he owes for it about $160, the
ballance I think could be had in reasonable
time. He requests you to write to me your
views on the subject, as clearly as may be
and he will send to me by a friend to know
the result. I made a very particular enquiry of him
of your character, and his feeling on the subject
of the return &c. He is married to a good woman
and family of cculer he has three children, and
was affectionate to them when I knew him
and industrious while here in an unusual degree

6b. Letter 1

The separation from his family must be
painfull. — I have given him this advice
& as nearly as I can recollect in these words,
"William, it may be even misfortune to be
born a Slave — but so we are by the Law
which we are bound to support — If you do
not wish to return, you ought in all
good conscience to remunerate for your time
all in your power." He said he would but
could not think of returning — & in this view
of the situation it would be improper for
me to say anything on the subject of
humanity, interest, and all the et ceteras,
the common topics on such occasions.
I will conclude by stating & I think if
you are disposed — a sum of between 2 & 300
dollars, say 230 or 40, may be had — or it is
in his power to control — and if you will
then name your agent, or fix on a place
I think he will come to the extent of his
power. — I am with respect &c
                         Abel Catlin

6c. Letter 1

Abel Catlin[1], Litchfield Ct, Spt 2d 1823
        to
Joseph Burrows, Esquire
        at the late firm of Burrows and Sturges[2]
            Savannah, Geo. now in N York

    Sir, William Grimes, who lived several years in this place
called on me yesterday and stated, the interview which he
had with you in New Haven, which drew forth the
circumstances of his leaving Sav[3] and the manner in which he
passed from Virginia &e which was before unknown, I believe
in this place. At his request I write you, and state, what he
proposes to be willing to do, and what, I believe he can, that
is, to surrender every thing in his power for his freedom. He
has property in this place which I think may be worth 4 or 400
fifty dollars, he owes for it about $160 — the balance I think
could be had in reasonable time. He requests you to write to
me your views on the subject, as early as may be and he will
send to me by a friend to know the result. I made a very
particular enquiry of him or your character, and his feeling
on the subject of the return, &c. He is married to a <u>good
woman and family of couler</u> he has three children, and was
affectionate to them when I knew him and industrious while
here in an unusual degree.

    The separation from his family must be painful. I have
given him this advice nearly, as I can recollect, in these words.
"William, it may be your misfortune to be born a Slave — but
so you was by the Laws which we are bound to support. If you
do not wish to return, you ought in all good conscience to

---

    1. Possibly Abel Catlin (b. 1770), a Litchfield, CT, physician.
    2. Burroughs and Sturges were a successful cotton and
commission firm in Savannah, GA.
    3. Savannah.

6d. Letter 1 transcription (above and facing)

remunerate for your time all in your power." He said he would but could not think of returning. In this view of the situation it would be improper for me to say anything, on the subject of humanity, interest and all the etceteras, the common topic on such occasions.

I will conclude by stating I think if you are disposed a sum of between 2 & 300 dollars, say 230 or 40, may be had — as it is in his power to control — and if you will [indecipherable] name your agent as for a place I think he will come to the extent of his power.

I am with respect &e
Abel Catlin

New York 1 Sept 1823

Abel Catlin Esqr
Litchfield   D Sir   Your favour of the 2 Inst

is recd & contents noticed, when I was at new haven
Grimes the property of Mr J. H. Welman called on me
& proferred to pay me $500 for his freedom, for this I
did offer to put him in possesion of a discharge —
all I can now say is If he will pay to Mr Wm H
Thompson, who I think is now in Litchfield $300
to come to be paid in 12 month the other $200 I will
see he recieves a full discharge if this can be done you
will please see Mr Thompson who will probably
leave your place in a very few days, show him this
letter (as I do not wright him) & his recpt will be a
satisfactory voucher — your letter I have sent Mr
Welman the owner of Grimes now in Alexd D C with
a coppy of this my reply — I shall leave this for Geo
in about 8 days if agreeable should be pleasd to hear
from you before my departure   Yours &c
                                             B B

7a. Letter 2

From B.B.[4] New York 6 Sept 1823
                        To
            Abel Catlin, Es., Litch.

D. Sir,
        Your favor of the 2 Inst[5] in recd' & contents noticed.
When I was at new haven Grimes the property of Mr. F. H.
Welman[6] called on me & proffered to pay me $500 for his
freedom, for this I did offer to put him in possession of a
discharge.

        All I can now say is If he will pay to Mr. Wm. H.
Thompson,[7] who I think is now in Litchfield $300 & secure to
be paid in 12 months the other $200 I will see he receives a full
discharge if this can be done you will please see Mr.
Thompson who will probably leave your place in a very few
days. show him this letter (as I do not wright him) & his
rect.[8] will be a satisfactory voucher. your letter I have sent
Mr. Welman the owner of Grimes now in Alexd D C[9] with a
copy of this my reply. I shall leave this for Geo[10] in about 8
days if agreeable should be pleased to hear from you before
my departure.

        Your. . . .
                BB

---

4. Benjamin Burroughs, business partner with Oliver Sturges
of Burroughs and Sturges.
5. September 2.
6. William Grimes's final owner, Francis Harvey Welman
(1780–1861), was a Savannah merchant.
7. William H. Thompson, a Litchfield merchant and debt
collector, acted as F. H. Welman's agent in the sale of William
Grimes.
8. Receipt.
9. Alexandria District of Columbia.
10. Georgia.

7b. Letter 2 transcription

Copy   Alexandria 16 Sept.r 1823

Abel Catlin Esquire

    D.r Sir

       Your letter of the 2.d instant to Mr.s Burroughs at New York & a Copy of his reply of the 5.th I have now before me on the subject of my petition with the assumed Name of Guerney, to which I should have replied some days ago had I not expected to have heard further from you: the offer made by Mr Burroughs to relieve my slave from slavery & which appears to him satisfactory, & afterwards confirmed in his letter to you, I hold myself in readiness to comply with provided it is fairly complied with, without putting me to further trouble & expense; although it is not by one half as much as he cost me, I feel myself bound to agree to it. the treatment I have had from this Negro is aggravating in the extreme; & when all the circumstances attending my owning him is known, you will readily assent to & which he will acknowledge; for I do believe notwithstanding his demands, he possesses honesty enough to come out with the truth; they are briefly these. Immediately after the Raid I purchased him of a Master White, who was about to sell him on a Plantation & from motives of pure benevolence & frequent solicitations & entreaties of his with tears in his eyes, I was overcome by feelings of humanity & bought him from his master with no apparent use for him, but purchased immediately, hired him as a House Servant & a Coachman on my return to Savannah in the fall: I clothed him well & gave him liberty to manage for himself in my absence & pay $3 p Week out of $50 p Month & which price he had hired himself, but to my astonishment on my return in the fall he had stoped mostly spent leaving me scarce one fourth of his wages on wondering & trifling amusements of his time to my use in his life. Mr Burroughs & myself & no advocate for slavery as you must perceive from our willingness to take a sum not much over half his value, for if I had him at Savannah under a good character I have no hesitation in saying he would command $800, but I never owned a Negro in my life for the purpose of traffick, nor yet will except Cunning I am compelled to do so in my own defence — If this arrangement can be made immediately with Mr.s Wm H Champion, (who Mr Burroughs

8b. Letter 3

T.H. Welman, Alexandria
To Wm. H. Thompson, Hartford
16 Sept 1823
Copy

Abel Catlin, Esquire

Dear Sir
    Your letter of the 2nd instant to Mr. Burroughs at New
York & a copy of his reply of the 6th I have now before me on
the subject of my Fellow with the assumed name of Grimey, to
which I should have replied some days ago had I not expected
to have heard further from you. The offer made by Mr.
Burroughs to relieve my slave from Slavery & which appears to
him satisfactory, & afterwards confirmed in his Letter to you, I
hold myself in readiness to comply with provided it is promptly
complied with, without putting me to further trouble &
expence; although it is not by one half as much as he cost me, I
feel myself bound to agree to it. The treatment I have rec. from
this negro is aggravating in the extreme, if when all the
circumstances attending my owning him is known, you will
readily assent to & which he will acknowledge. for I do believe
notwithstanding his conduct he posseses honesty enough to
come out with the truth; they are briefly these Immediately
after the [indecipherable] I purchased him of a doctor White
who was about to sell him on a Plantation & from motives of
pure benevolence & frequent solicitations & entreaties this with
tears in his eyes, I was overcome by feelings of humanity &
became his master with no apparent use for him, but concluded
I would employ him as a House Servt & a Coachman on my
return to Savannah in the Fall: I clothed him well and gave him
liberty to manage for himself in my absence & pay $3 per week
out of $30. p month and which [indecipherable] he had time
himself, but to my astonishment on my return in the Fall he
had eloped without even leaving me one cent of his wages or

even devoting one moment of his time to my use in his life. Mr. Burroughs or myself is no advocates for Slavery as you must perceive from our willingness to take a Sum not much over half his value, for if I had him at Savannah under a good character I have no hesitation in saying he would command $800, but I never owned a negro in my life for the purpose of traffick, nor yet will except I am compelled to do so in my own defence. If this arrangement can be made immediately with Mr. Wm. H Thompson, who Mr. Burroughs has named to you in the terms contained in his letter of the 6th Inst. I will execute the Papers here by your sending me Mr. Thompson's Rect; or if there is any doubt of a full & ample compliance you may Instruct my friend here to make the settlement with me in accordance to Mr. Burroughs [indecipherable] on my compliance. I shall leave this for Savannah by the 5th or 10th of next month but expect an answer from you by return mail. In the event of this arrangement being entered into with Mr. Thompson have the goodness to call on him on rect of this and show him this letter, as it is probable he may be about leaving Connecticut on his way to Savannah.

With much respect I am

Yours sincerely
T. H. Welman

PAID 25

William H. Thompson Esq.

Augusta.

Paid —

Georgia

9a. Letter 4

Littlefield Nov 8th 1823

Mr William Thompson

Sir

I hold in my hand a Note given by the flesh men I received of $550 in favour of _____ he wishes to have the avail of it _____ for his manumission and he requests me to ask as a favour that you will hold communication with Mr Wilmen on his behalf — and write the result to me — I feel though the Note might be cashed for $200 and that the _____ sum could be paid if he m. lies, by $100 p annum and interest kept clear. Sam has now gone with Cook to the W. Ind. I presume he will be back by the return Vessel, for I have no Idea, G. will 4 days _____

In great haste I subscribe myself
your very humble Servt
Abel Collins

9b. Letter 4

Litchfield Nov 3 1823

Abel Catlin, Litchfield
        to
William H. Thompson
        Augusta, Georgia

Sir,
        I hold in my hand a Note given by the black man I
received of $550 in favor of Grimes he wishes to have the avail
[?] of it go for his manumission and he requests me to ask as a
favor that you hold communication with Mr. Welman on his
behalf. and write the result to me. I [indecipherable] think the
Note might be cashed for $200 and [indecipherable] by $100 per
Annum and [indecipherable] I promise he will be back by the
[indecipherable]
        In great haste I subscribe myself your very humble Servt
                Abel Catlin

9c. Letter 4 transcription

Savannah 21st April 1824.

Wm. H. Thompson Esquire
        Dear Sir

        Herewith I hand you my power of atty
& Execute proper & Sufficient Papers for the freedom of our fellow
Theodore in the Event of your being able to obtain a Sufficient Sum
_____ for which I shall leave to your discretion & be satisfied
with any Settlement you may make that in your Judgment you may
deem for my Interest — To Enable you to make up your Mind
_____ the Remuneration he is willing to make of which Mr.
Burroughs may willing to Accede to this Summer: I enclose you
all the Communications that has passed between Mr. Catlin (The
Guardian of Theodore) to Mr Burroughs, yourself & myself I leave it to
be for you to determine believing you will do all that is Right & what
is my duty to agree to. With much Respect believe me to be

                    Yours Sincerely
                    P. H. Thomas

Savannah 21st April 1824

Mr. William H. Thompson, Esquire
      Dear Sir
              Herewith I hand you my power of Atty to execute
proper & sufficient Papers for the freedom of my fellow
Theodore in the Event of your being able to obtain a sufficient
remuneration, of which I shall leave to your discretion & be
satisfied with any Settlement you may make that in your
[indecipherable] you may deem for my Interest. to Enable you
to make up your mind in [indecipherable] perceive the
remuneration he is willing to make of which Mr. Burroughs
was willing to accede to last Summer: I enclose you all the
Communications that has passed between Mr. Catlin (the
Guardian of Theodore) to Mr. Burroughs, Yourself & myself I
leave it for you to determine believing you will do all that is
right & what is my [indecipherable] to agree to.

      With much respect believe me to be
          Yours sincerely, T. H. Welman

10b. Letter 5 transcription

11. Gravestone of William and Clarissa Grimes located in the historic Grove Street Cemetery across from Yale University, New Haven, Connecticut. (Courtesy of R. Kyle Brown)

12. This program announces a fundraiser for the Elliott Literary Institute Library Fund held on July 30, 1875, in the Young Men's U. B. Society's Hall in San Francisco. Mrs. Cecelia Williams, daughter of William and Clarissa Grimes, is billed as the "Eminent Tragedienne." (J. B. Sanderson Collection, the Bancroft Library, University of California, Berkeley)

I will here mention that during my passage I lay concealed as much as possible: some evenings I would crawl out and go and lie down with the sailors on deck; the night being dark, the captain could not distinguish me from the hands, having a number on board of different complexions. He, or some one, would often in the night, when there was something to be done, come on deck and call, forward, there, boy! Aye, aye, sir, was the reply; then they would be immediately at their posts, I remaining on the floor, not perceived by him.

We cast off from the wharf at Savannah Saturday night, and remained in the Savannah river until Monday morning; we then crossed the bar near the light-house. After we had got into the ocean the sailors gave three hearty cheers, and gave me to understand that I was clear; we were out of sight of land, they said. Nothing more of any consequence occurred until we arrived at the Quarantine Ground, New York. I remained concealed from the captain, mate and steward until after we arrived.

One morning after I left my place of concealment, and was in the forecastle of the vessel intending to change my clothes, as I was putting on a clean shirt, the mate came down, (the captain and passengers having gone before to New York;) he perceived me with my shirt half on (being so frightened that I stood motionless,) said, why, Grimes, how came you here? I could make him no answer. He then called some of the crew and inquired of them how I came there. They replied, poor fellow, he stole aboard. He then inquired if the steward knew that I was aboard. I told him that he did not. He replied, know well that you do not let him know it. He then inquired if the captain knew it. I answered him, no, sir. He then said to me, let no one know anything about it; I wish that I myself knew nothing of it. Here, boys, put him over the bows, and set him ashore on Staten Island.

Upon that, one of the sailors took me ashore in the boat. On landing he found another sailor with whom he was acquainted, and told him my circumstances, requesting him to assist me in getting to New York. He promised him that he would. After staying on the island a few hours, this man told me to follow him down to the river where the packet-boat[66] lay, as she would sail soon. There being some of the crew

---

66. In the nineteenth century, "packet-boat" referred to various-sized ships designed to transport mail, goods, and passengers on regularly scheduled routes.

on board the Casket sick, it was necessary that all who passed from the island, having been on board of her, and all other persons who went from the island to New York, should be examined by a doctor stationed there for that purpose. This was what I most feared. This man had once spoken to the doctor, and his name entered on the book; the doctor stood on the wharf to receive the names of all those who passed into the packet, and none to pass without giving their names, the same to be recorded in his book, which he held in his hand.

As we approached the wharf, I felt as if my heart was in my mouth, or, in other words, very much afraid that I should be compelled to give my name, together with an account from whence I came, and where I was going, and in what manner I came there. To all this I should not dare to answer, (fearing in one case to implicate the master of the vessel in which I came, who was perfectly innocent, and in the second, of being taken and again returned to my master, there to remain in slavery during the rest of my life;) but I followed him down to the packet-boat. I perceived the doctor had his head turned a little to the left, looking at something in that direction. He perceived the sailor who was my conductor, and recognized him as one he had examined; but, not noticing me, I slipped aboard without being interrogated at all.

I was in the greatest fear of being detected, so much so that I almost fainted; but when I heard the word given to push off, I rejoiced heartily. I then told the sailor, who had been my friend, that I was convinced I should meet with some person on my landing whom I had formerly known. He replied, never mind that, take hold of my chest, and come along with me. I did so, and soon after we arrived at the lodgings of this sailor, who proved to be my friend (which I made my place of abode for the present.) In the course of the afternoon I saw a colored girl in the street near the house. I inquired of her if she would walk with me a little ways, in order to see the town, and that I could again find my lodgings. I being a stranger there, was afraid of being lost.

We walked about the city some time; at length, as we were walking up Broadway, who should I see but Mr. Oliver Sturges, of Fairfield, who once had been my master in Savannah. To my great astonishment, he came up to me, and said, why, Theodore, how came you here? I lied to him, and told him I had been there about two weeks; being so frightened, I knew not what to say, never intending to tell a lie, wilfully or maliciously. He asked me how all things were going on at his yard in Savannah. I answered, all well, I just came from there, sir. After a few moments conversation, he passed on one way, and I went on towards my lodgings, where I rested that night.

The next morning, after purchasing a loaf of bread and a small piece of meat, I started on foot for New Haven.[67] I could often get an opportunity to ride; sometimes behind the stage, at others, I could sometimes persuade a teamster to take me on for a short distance. In this manner, I arrived at New Haven. After I arrived there, and even before, every carriage or person I saw coming behind me, I fancied were in pursuit of me. Lying still on board the vessel so long, made it fatiguing for me to walk far at a time without stopping to rest; my situation there being quite confined, and no opportunity for exercise. I often was obliged to go off the road and lie down for some time; and whenever I saw any person coming on, that I suspected, I took that opportunity for a resting spell, and went out of sight until they passed by. Finding my money growing short, I found that I must live prudent. I met a couple of boys on the road who had some apples. I bought them, which, together with what little provision I took with me, was all I had to subsist on until I arrived at New Haven, which was three days. I lodged the two nights I was on the road at private houses.

When I arrived at New Haven, I found that all the money I had left amounted to no more than seventy-five cents. That night I lodged at a boarding house, kept by a certain Mrs. W., who took me to be a white man; and although I have lived in New Haven since that time a number of years, she never knew to this day but what it was a white man that lodged there that night. The next morning I went to work for Abel Lanson,[68] who kept a livery stable. He set me at work in a ledge of rocks, getting out stone for building. This I found to be the hardest work I had ever done, and began to repent that I had ever come away from Savannah, to this hard cold country.

---

67. New Haven, Connecticut, is approximately halfway between New York City and Boston on the coast of the Long Island Sound.

68. Abel Lanson, brother of William Lanson, was a prominent African American landowner and businessman in New Haven. The Lanson brothers owned a livery stable and were important hostlers in New Haven in the 1820s.

After I had worked at this for about three months, I got employment in taking care of a sick person, who called his name Carr, who had been a servant to Judge Clay,[69] of Kentucky; he was then driving for Lanson. I took care of him, and took his place for some time. One day, as I was assisting Isaac (a son of Lanson) to harness a horse, to my great astonishment and surprise, master Stephen Bullock, whom I have heretofore mentioned, as the relation to, and superintendent of my master's office in Savannah, came up to me and said, why, John, it is as hot here as in Savannah. (I will here mention, that as it may appear strange for me to have so many names, to those who are not acquainted with the circumstance, that it is a practice among the slave holders, whenever one buys a slave of another, if the name does not suit him, or if he has one of the same name already, he gives him what name he pleases. I, for these reasons, have had three different names.) I was so much surprised to see Mr. Bullock, that I could scarce give him an answer. He spoke to me several times. I was so much afraid and astonished, that I could give him no answer. I was afraid he would ask me how I came in New Haven.

Who can express my feelings at first seeing him? I behaved so bashful and afraid to speak, that after saying a few words he walked down Church street, and I saw no more of him. After he had gone, Isaac said to me, why, he appears to know you. I replied, yes, it is no wonder that he knows me. I then went and informed my friends that I had seen my young master, and I did not think it prudent for me to stay in New Haven long.

Accordingly I left town, and went on to a place called Southington, a few miles back in the country, where I went to work on a farm. Here an accident befel me, which I will mention. I one day went to assist Capt. Potter to pick up apples, and having on a red flannel shirt, the cattle were afraid of it as I was attempting to take them from the cart. Having stepped between them, in order to let the tongue of the cart down, which was filled with apples, they started and ran down a hill as fast as they possibly could. I held on to the tongue of the cart as long as I had strength enough. They were constantly kicking me in the face. I durst

69. "Judge Clay" may refer to Henry Clay (1777–1852), a U.S. senator from Kentucky.

not attempt to quit my hold, fearing I should be crushed to pieces by the loaded cart; but not being able to hold on any longer, after they had run down the hill, and through a pair of bars, I fell, and the cart passed over me and crushed my ancle severely. The neighbors gathered round me, expecting every moment to see me breathe my last. They took me up and carried me to a house, sent for a doctor, and he came. I being so much bruised and kicked, the blood was streaming from me in many places. The Doctor soon stopped it, and bound up my ancle.

I recovered slowly, and was obliged to crawl on my hands and knees a great while, and supported myself on what little money I had acquired, until I procured a pair of crutches. I then used to go around amongst the neighbors in Southington, husking corn, and doing such kind of work as I could do in my situation. I found it much harder at this time to be a free man, than I had to be a slave; but finally got to be able to earn fifty cents per day. After I had so far recovered as to be able to walk, or rather limp without crutches, I returned to New Haven. After staying there a short time, I was taken sick, and continued unable to work for a week or two. I put up with Abel Lanson, and assisted him in digging a well. I then worked about the Colleges,[70] cutting wood, at which I earned about one dollar a day, of which I was very saving, until I had collected about twenty dollars.

I then left New Haven and started for Providence,[71] where I spent the chief part of my money. I then went into partnership with a man by the name of Boham, and kept a barber's shop. After a few months, we dissolved partnership. I then went on to Newport,[72] and after waiting some time for a passage to New Bedford,[73] at length found a packet bound for that port; but the wind blowing very hard, I did not think it safe to go on board, so I put my trunk on board and went on, myself

70. Yale College and New Haven Law School, which later became Yale Law School in 1824.

71. Providence, one hundred miles north of New Haven, is the capital of Rhode Island.

72. Newport, thirty-five miles south of Providence, is on the Rhode Island coast.

73. New Bedford, Massachusetts, thirty miles northeast of Newport, was a major whaling port in the nineteenth century.

on foot, it being thirty miles, and arrived there before the packet. I had not money sufficient to pay for my board one week. Wishing to get a place to work so as soon as I could, and hearing that Mr. John Howland wanted a servant, I applied to him for employ; we soon struck a bargain at the rate of nine dollars a month; this was in June. In the fall after, I kept shop for myself some part of the time; the rest part I worked for Mr. Howland, until it began to grow cold. I also kept a few groceries.

The colored people being often in there evenings, had finally got so much habituated to take to their own heads in rioting and carousing, (which I endeavored to suppress in vain,) that Mr. Hazzet, my landlord, asked me a number of times if I had not better give up the shop. To which I replied, yes, sir, I will very gladly, for I see the colored people have imposed upon me. I being a stranger, and the only barber in the place, except white people, they would often come in with their families and dance evenings, until late; and being noisy and riotous, I would endeavor to stop them, but to no purpose; they still persisted in it, until I was obliged to give up my shop.

There was a woman who lived in the room below me: she kept house there, and was not pleased with the noise, saying she would not have it there. I suppose she complained to my landlord, and for that reason I was obliged to give up my shop. After one quarter, I did it, and paid him up my rent. After I had left the shop about two months, this woman[74] was heard to cry murder in the night. The neighbors immediately assembled, when two sailors were seen to escape out of her window, go down on to the wharf, and go on board a vessel. The morning following, the authority made enquiry about it. On questioning her, she said that two persons came into her room and offered her violence; she resisted as long as her strength held out, and after they had accomplished their design, they then abused and whipped her until she made the outcry.

74. *The New Bedford Mercury* reported that Elizabeth Bly was the victim of this break-in and attack. William Grimes was deemed a suspect on account of his supposed desire for "revenge for some trivial cause." The *Mercury* claims that Grimes was arrested for the crime but was later acquitted by "Justice Williams" because of insufficient evidence. When Bly testified that she feared further bodily harm, Grimes was again arrested and placed in the Taunton Jail. Later he was acquitted a second time. There are no extant official court records of this case.

They [the New Haven authorities] then enquired of her if she knew who it was. She replied, no. They then enquired, do you suspect any one. She said, no. On enquiring again if she had any reason to mistrust any one, on any account, she replied, I know of no one who owes me a grudge except William Grimes. Whilst he lived in this house, over my room, he used to have a great deal of noise there, which disturbed me; I said considerable about it, which was the means of his quitting his shop. He then threatened to be revenged for it. I can think of no other person.

I was then taken before a Justice, Esq. Williams, to answer to this charge. I proved by Mr. John Howland, Jr., to whom I had hired out for the winter, for seven dollars a month, that I was in his house all that night. He knew me to go to bed, and as a light snow was then falling, he said it was impossible for me to go out of the house without his knowledge. After three days' time I was discharged, they not being able to prove anything against me. Before I left the room, I was again arrested and taken to this woman's room, where they questioned her very close. They asked her if she could or would swear to the voice of the person or persons that had been seen to come out of her window. She replied, no, I cannot. They then asked her if she was willing to swear that she was afraid of her life. She answered, yes. I was again taken back to the court for another trial; I was well convinced that the woman knew it was not me, and also knew who it was.

Esq. Williams asked me if I would have a lawyer. I not knowing what to answer, never having been brought up in a court before, answered, yes, sir, I will have you for my lawyer. He replied, I am bound to do you all the good I can; I must do justice. You had better get some other attorney; but there being no one handy, they (my opponents) said, as you have no attorney, we will have none. Esq. Williams then said to me, you must be recognized together with some other person in the sum of $300, for your appearance at Taunton[75] court, in about three months. I not being acquainted with any person to whom I wished to apply, and having no money, I therefore went to jail, where I stayed until the court set. When the trial came on, two witnesses were brought forward, who testified

---

75. Located in Taunton, Massachusetts, twenty-three miles north of New Bedford and twenty miles northeast of Providence.

that they heard me say I would injure the woman. The Judge enquired of them, was that all you heard? is that all you know? They answered, yes. He then acquitted me, cautioning me to behave myself well.

I then went directly to Providence, where I remained a few days, then continued on to Norwich,[76] where I went to work for a few weeks, for Mr. Christopher Starr. From thence I went to New London,[77] where I purchased a set of barber's tools. Having been informed previous to this that a barber might do well at Stonington Point, after crossing the river I pursued my journey, it being through woods. I had not gone more than one or two miles before I saw four or five men, who made directly towards me. I was very much frightened when I saw them, but could not tell why. I was much more so, when they came up to me and said, where are you going, boy? I answered them to Stonington Point. Where did you come from? I came from New London. What have you got there in your bundle? I have got nothing but some barber's tools. You are a barber then, are you? Yes, I was told that Stonington Point was a good place for a barber, and I purchased a set of tools in New London, with the intention of going there to establish a shop. They then replied, there has lately been a store broken open, and we are now in pursuit of the rogues; we have orders to search every person we meet with; we are therefore under the necessity of searching you. I replied, you may search me gentlemen, if you please. They then proceeded to search my bundle, and finding nothing more there than I had told them, let me go on; but advised me not to go there: that the people were not civil, but would raise the devil with any person who should undertake to establish a barber's shop there. They advised me to return back to Mr. Starr's: and after considerable conversation I resolved to return; which I did, and worked on Mr. Starr's farm about two weeks longer.

I then went to New London, and took the steamboat for New Haven, where I arrived some time in May. I then went to work about the Colleges, as I had formerly done; also, shaving, cutting hair, &c., such as waiting on the scholars in their rooms, and all other kinds of work that I could do when not employed at this. I worked about the Colleges,

---

76. Norwich, Connecticut, is fifty miles southwest of Providence.
77. New London is fifteen miles south of Norwich on the Connecticut coast.

about six or eight months. I had then accumulated about fifty dollars, and bearing that there was no barber in Litchfield, (a very pleasant town, about thirty-six miles back in the country, where the celebrated Law School, under the direction of Tapping Reeve,[78] Esq., was kept,) and as there were between twenty and thirty law students, I thought it a good place for me. I accordingly went and established myself as a barber. I very soon had a great deal of custom, amounting to fifty or sixty dollars per month. After I had resided there for about a year with about as good success, I undertook to keep one or two horses and gigs[79] to let. For some time I made money very fast; but at length trading horses a number of times, the horse jockies would cheat me, and to get restitution I was compelled to sue them. I would sometimes win the case; but the lawyers would alone reap the benefit of it. At other times I lost my case, fiddle and all; besides paying my Attorney.

Let it not be imagined that the poor and friendless are entirely free from oppression where slavery does not exist: this would be fully illustrated if I should give all the particulars of my life, since I have been in Connecticut. This I may do in a future edition, and when I feel less delicacy about mentioning names.

While at Litchfield I sold a wagon to a neighbor and took a note, which I was compelled to sue. My debtor lived in a house with another man, whom I had made my enemy, by dunning him in the street for cutting his hair. They out of revenge went to a Grand Juror and made complaint against me for keeping a bad girl at my house. I always kept a girl, as we took in washing, and this girl who had been living with an inhabitant there, my wife hired about ten days before. The trial was before Squire M. who got another Esq. to sit with him, and a great court it was too.

They asked me if I had a lawyer. I said I would plead my own case, as I was sure they had nothing against me. I however told one of Judge G.'s sons that he might answer for me if he was a mind to. There were a great

78. Tapping Reeve, brother-in-law of Aaron Burr, established the nation's first recognized law school in his home in 1774. The Litchfield Law School educated many of the young nation's leaders, including two vice presidents and many congressmen. Litchfield, Connecticut, is forty-five miles north of New Haven.

79. A light two-wheeled, one-horse carriage.

many of the inhabitants summoned to testify, and all of them testified in my favor except *two*. The jail-keeper who lived second door from me, said he knew nor heard nothing against me; and he was no friend of mine. Trowbridge and Hungerford said they had heard thus and so: but were not questioned where they got their information. If I had plead my own case, I could have done better than any lawyer or rather student. M. Smith managed the case against me. Esq., one of the court as before mentioned by invitation, in giving his opinion, made a long speech against me; or rather, he said there was proof enough that such report was enough to convict me; he said more than the lawyer against me. I had got most of my business by activity, from his servant, who, before I went to Litchfield, was the principal waiter, &c., for the students. I thought this trial showed his master, and some others thought as much of this as of the crime of which I was accused; particularly as it was one at which they were not likely to feel much indignation in their hearts. The girl was of a bad character; but I did not know it. She was white. I sent her away as soon as I heard anything against her. I asked my lawyer why he did not question the witness against me, where they heard reports; and he said there was nothing proved against me. The court, he said, did as they was a mind to. I being a negro, I suppose they thought no one would ever notice it. I had money, and if I had not, the town *would* have to pay the cost. I say before my God, that I was convicted of keeping a bad house when I had only kept this girl in my house ten days, and knew nothing but that she was virtuous.

I was warned out of town shortly after I went to Litchfield by one of the Selectmen, and through the influence of this servant before mentioned or his friends. But I went to Esq. B. who told them to let me stay, and I heard no more about it. After I was put under bonds, I was obliged to give a mortgage of my house; and this same trial was five hundred dollars damage to me; it injured my character of course, and those who suppose I have no feelings are mistaken.

A few days after my trial I went down to cut the Governor's hair,[80] and he said to me, Grimes, I am sorry that you got in such a scrape.

---

80. Oliver Wolcott, Jr. (1760–1833) was a native of Litchfield and was educated at Yale College and Litchfield Law School. He later served as governor of Connecticut from 1817 to 1826.

I suppose his since Secretary would persuade him that I was guilty. I only said I was not guilty; and I do wish that the Governor only did know the truth about it. I after this met Esq. B. in the street, and he said, William, they did not do you justice at the trial. I talked with him, and he told me when the county court set, he would get the bonds taken off if the State's Attorney did not object; but the Attorney did object at the instigation of ———.

This servant had been tried for the same offence which I had, and was convicted; but found friends. I presume if I had been actually guilty, I should have met with different treatment.

It has been my fortune most always to be suspected by the good, and to be cheated and abused by the vicious. An instance of rascality I will now mention, which took place at Litchfield: one J. swapped horses with me, and by fraud induced me to give twenty dollars to boot. The horse I swapped cost me five. I sold the horse I had of him for fifteen dollars. I sued him though, and recovered, I believe thirty dollars.[81] I bought a mare of one P. and paid him good money. Afterwards he came to me with a counterfeit bill, and said I paid it to him. I knew I did not, for it was torn and ragged. He threatened me and I took it, being ignorant of the law. But I understand the law now, pretty well, at least that part which consists in paying *fees*. My case with the horse jockey cost me a great deal of money. It was curious to hear his witnesses testify: some who knew nothing about the horse or the bargain swore just as if they were reciting their catechism. God help them! One of my children was sick, and I sold a buffalo skin to the physician while he was visiting the child, for which he gave me six dollars. Before I left Litchfield I could not get him to make out his bill: but after I went to New Haven, this doctor sent his bill down there for collection. I thought I had paid enough, and refused paying any more than the six dollars, unless he swore to his account. This he did, but what was strange, he went up into Tolland County, about forty miles off, to do it. I was in as good credit as any man in Litchfield, and as good a paymaster. Quackery and extortion generally go together.

---

81. Litchfield County court records report that the case of *William Grimes v. Horace Johnson* was filed on May 29, 1819, but not settled until January 14, 1820. The court found in favor of Grimes and ordered Johnson to pay him thirty dollars for the sale of a diseased mare.

I used to carry to the students' rooms their meals when they wanted. One of them from Charleston, a graduate of Yale College, sent for his dinner one day. I carried a variety of dishes, a very large dinner, and a plenty of wine and brandy. He had several gentlemen in the room with him that day, and they did all sit down at the table, and they would have me sit down to the table too. One of them would say, Mr. Grimes, a glass of wine with you, sir; and the next gentleman would say the same, and so they kept on, until I had got two glasses to their one all round the table. I began to feel myself on a footing with them, and made as free with them as they did with me, and drank to them, and they would set me to making speeches. They not only drank with me themselves, until they got me as drunk as a fool, but they called in Peter Hamden, who was going along, and made him drink a glass of brandy and water with me. At last I took the floor and lay there speechless some hours. I had two or three apprentice boys; towards night, they came after me and led me home. I never was so drunk in my life before. I looked so like death, my wife[82] was shocked at the sight of me.

Harry, the servant I have mentioned before, as my great rival and enemy, I knew kept a lewd house. His protector had been so active in the prosecution against me, that I thought I would retaliate a little. I went to a grand juror therefore, and made a complaint against Harry. The grand juror did not understand managing the case at all, as he was just appointed. The trial was before Esquire B. Mr. Beers managed the case for Harry, and got him clear; the witnesses being all Harry's friends. And when a lawyer makes a justice, the justice sometimes is very apt to remember his creator. Harry then turned round and sued me for damages in getting him complained of. He employed two lawyers, Mr. Sanford and Mr. Beers,[83] and I employed two. Before I made complaint against Harry, I was riding in the stage with a man to New

82. Clarissa Caesar (1799–1868) was the daughter of Trial and Timothy Caesar. Her father served in Humphrey's all-black militia during the Revolutionary War.

83. David C. Sanford (b. 1798) practiced law in Litchfield and New Milford, Connecticut. He was later elected Superior Court Judge in New Milford. Seth P. Beers (b. 1781) attended Litchfield Law School (1803–05) and then practiced law in that town.

Haven, who told me all about Harry's house. I now went to New Haven, and took this man's deposition before Esquire Dennison.[84] At the trial, which made some noise in Litchfield, we called on Harry's lawyers to give bonds, which they did, and at it they went until dinner, when the court adjourned. Only one of Harry's lawyers returned after dinner, and all he did was to pay the cost and be off. So I came off triumphant.

At one time while I was living in New Haven, I applied to the jail keeper in Litchfield, to borrow two hundred dollars. He said if I would buy his horse and cutter,[85] he would let me have fifty dollars cash, and I must give my note for two hundred dollars, with a mortgage on my place for security. I did so. The horse and cutter I suppose was worth seventy-five dollars. But while my ignorance thus exposed me to imposition, it was perhaps the only way in which I could learn wisdom; indeed, those to whom I have done kindness, have often proved ungrateful. One Barnes I recollect was confined in Litchfield jail for the fine and cost which had been imposed for a fighting scrape. He told me if I would pay it, which was twelve dollars, he would let me have his cow to get my pay. I paid it, gave him some change after I had taken him out, and shaved him, so that he might go home and see his wife. But I found the cow was not his. His brother is a cabinet maker and rich, but would not help him, I believe.

I got into a quarrel with a student. He struck me in a passion and I sued. He gave me twenty dollars, and I settled it; and having about this time an opportunity to let my place, I did so. The rent was seventy dollars a year. My object was to go to New Haven, which I now did. I hired a place of Esquire Daggett[86] in New Haven, close by the Colleges, and gave him one hundred dollars rent. I kept a victualing shop, and waited

84. Charles Denison was an attorney in New Haven.
85. A small sleigh, usually drawn by a single horse.
86. David Daggett (1764–1851) graduated from Yale College and practiced law in New Haven. He served as Justice and then as Chief Justice on the Connecticut State Supreme Court (1826–32; 1832–34) and as major of New Haven (1828). As an advocate for states' rights and African colonization, Daggett publicly opposed both emancipation and education for African Americans. In 1831, he helped draft a local resolution against the formation of a "negro college" in New Haven.

on the students. I kept money to let, and soon got into full business. I bought furniture too of the students; in this my business interfered with Mr. E. my next neighbor, which brought upon me his displeasure. In fact, I had such a run of custom, that all the shop keepers, that is of the huckster shops[87] about college, and who get their living out of the students, fell upon me, to injure me in every possible manner; they had more sense than I had about keeping in with the Faculty, and others about there, but I can swear they were not more honest in my opinion. They took pains to prejudice the college steward[88] against me.

When I wanted wood, I used to get some student who owed me, to sign a bill and then get the wood delivered at my house; the wood is furnished by [the] college to the students. This was the only way in which I could get my pay often. I had got a load at my house, which had been delivered in this manner. The carman had thrown it part off, when the steward came up and ordered him to carry it back. I ordered him to unload. He began to put the wood back, when I seized him and stopped it. The steward says you rascal, this is my wood, and are you not going to give up? I said I am not, it is in my possession. He took back, however, what was not thrown off. But I went immediately up to the steward's office and demanded it again, and told him I would sue him if he did not restore it; and he gave it up. I told him that it was all I could get from the student. The steward knew if I sued him it would make a great noise and laugh about town, and he knew, (being a lawyer,) that I could recover. Being in opposition to all these fellows who get their living about college, they all hated me, and would go to the Tutors[89] and throw out insinuations against me, would tell the students if they had me in their rooms, they would be suspected. But notwithstanding their efforts, I did a mighty good business.

As I have spoken of a wife, it may seem strange that I have not related the tale of love which must have preceded matrimony. It would

87. A store that sells small wares.

88. In the nineteenth century, Yale College stewards provided food for the commons and cleaned student rooms.

89. Yale tutors were usually recent graduates pursing professional studies. They typically held this teaching position for a few years before moving on to advanced work in their chosen fields.

be indelicate to relate many things, necessary to a full understanding of a courtship, from beginning to end. One might tell how he got acquainted; whether he was welcomed or repulsed at first. Praise his wife's beauty, or commend her temper before the die is cast. Somehow I did not like, did not know how to tell it. I got married. Though before I went to Litchfield to live, and shortly after I returned to New Haven from Taunton, as is mentioned before, I used to hear students say something about taking Yankee girls for wives, and I thought I would look round and see I if I could not find one. I had a great many clothes from the students, and I could rig myself up mighty well. And I have always seen that the girls seemed to like those best who dressed the finest. Yet I do reckon the generality of girls are sluttish, though my wife is not. When a servant, and since too, I have seen so much behind the curtain, that I don't want told. I recollect one student telling a story of this sort, when I was in the room. An acquaintance of his had been courting a lady some time, and I forget how it was exactly, but after he married her, come to see her in the morning, with all the curls, ribbons, combs, caps, earrings, wreaths, &c. &c. stripped off, he did not know her.

While I was looking round, I found a plain looking girl in New Haven, and I found she was the very one Providence had provided for me; though her beauty, before it faded, and her figure before it was spoiled, as it always must be soon, were such as a fine Virginian like myself, might be proud to embrace. I paid my attention to her. I loved her into an engagement. After a while I got one of the students to write a publishment, and sent it to the Rev. Mr. M.;[90] he did not read it the next Sabbath, as was customary, and I went to see him. He said he would read it next Sunday, though he thought it was a hoax. So next Sunday he made proclamation. I was then married in the Episcopal Manner. I reckon my wife did belong, originally, at Middlebury, twenty miles from New Haven.

I had at that time become much alarmed about being taken up and carried back to my master, which was one reason why I left New Haven for Litchfield. My wife's mother came down to see her, and she went home with her, and came down in a wagon after me, and as I was walking

---

90. Reverend Samuel Merwin, a pastor in the interdenominational United Society, married William Grimes and Clarissa Caesar on August 18, 1817.

in the street that evening she came, I thought I heard the constable after me, and Mr. Sturges, who formerly owned me. I heard them say, the constable and another, that fellow ran away from Savannah. I was so frightened my strength left me. But I began to run. I stopped at Lanson's, and left word for my wife, and then went on as swift as a deer, over the fences. I never thought where I was going. I traveled until two or three o'clock. Oh, how the sweat did run off me! I crept into a barn and slept; and the next day I arrived at Middlebury. Here I went to work among the farmers, until I left for Litchfield, as afore mentioned, and commenced my barber shop and waiting. I suppose I staid at Litchfield, four years, until when I rented my house, and came to New Haven, as above stated.

While living in New Haven, one C. a student, gave me a room in the house where he roomed, and I waited on him. He sent me to the College Hall after his breakfast. Mr. Kennedy, one of the cooks, ordered me out, and we had considerable of a scrumage[91] in the Hall, but I got the breakfast. I told Corbett, and he advised me to sue him. I went to lawyer Thomas, and got a writ drawn, and had it served that day. Mr. Kennedy got Mr. Twining[92] for his attorney; indeed I think he had two lawyers. I lost my case. They had President Dwight's[93] deposition, who stated that he put these men in the hall to do for him as they would in their own houses. Therefore, Kennedy had according to law, a right to put me out. I was at this time a stranger in New Haven, but I knew a great many of the students, and they were very good to me. They paid the cost of this case, or gave me clothes and money, so that I made money, if anything by the suit.

My acquaintance among the black people were friendly to me in New Haven, and it is no more than just that I should preserve the name of one of them, who is now dead, from oblivion, particularly as he was

---

91. Probably a "scrimmage," meaning a fight or tussle.

92. Stephen Twining graduated from Yale in 1795 and practiced law in New Haven. He was also a steward of Yale College from 1819 to 1832.

93. Although there is no extant record of this fight in Yale president Timothy Dwight's minutes (he became ill shortly after this period and died in February 1817), contemporary college rules confirm that students were prohibited from sending anyone to the commons to remove food or property without the permission of a professor, a tutor, or the president himself.

a runaway slave, like myself and very distinguished in his profession. As soon as I came from New Bedford to New Haven, I went up to College to see Barber Thompson, and to see how he came on; and I found him very sick. He was very glad to see me, and gave the shop into my possession, to keep for him. Barber Thompson, for that was the name he went by in New Haven, was a slave to Mr. Benly, of Port Royal, Va. He came on to the north with a gentleman, to wait on him, and ran away during the last war. He was honest and clever, was called the greatest barber in America, kept shop by the College, and was often called to officiate at parties and weddings, being the politest servant in town. He died last winter, and I had him buried in my burying ground.

That poverty which often leaves my wife and children without a supper, may well excuse me for leaving his grave nameless. A stone I intended to erect with this epitaph:

> Here lies old Thompson! And how he is dead,
> I think some one should tell his story;
> For while men's faces must be shaved,
> His name should live in glory.

But I have not for the reason above, put up a stone.

The enmity of some of my rivals in business, led them to make misrepresentations about town against my character, and one of them had some authority in town affairs. My conduct was good, and the strict laws of Connecticut could find nothing to punish; but the selectmen have power to warn any man out of town who has not gained a settlement,[94] which is a difficult thing for a poor man. This was the only course my enemies could take with me. There was certainly no danger of my coming upon the town,[95] which is all the object of the law to prevent. It is

94. To satisfy the requirements of the New England Settlement Act of 1796, one had to prove financial independence for a period of six years or more. Such proof provided the legal right to settle in a town.

95. "Coming upon the town": becoming dependent on public support. Town selectmen, after obtaining a warrant, had the authority to remove from the town anyone who could not prove a legal "settlement." The selectment could also impose a weekly fine on the offender.

very mean and cruel to drive a man out of town because he is suspected of some crime or breach of law. If he is guilty, punish him, but not set him adrift on suspicion, or from mere tyranny, because his poverty exposes him to it. If I was a pimp why not punish me for it, not warn a man out of town, because his enemies accuse him of crime. Such was the fact though. They then brought a suit for the penalty, one dollar and sixty-seven cents a week. The suit was before a justice in Woodbridge.[96] I saw him in town and told him I wished to have the case adjourned to New Haven. They got judgment against me, as I did not appear. I was then in this predicament, liable to be whipped at the post, if I did not pay the fine or depart in ten days. I think I should not have left, but paid my dollar and sixty-seven cents a week and staid, if I had not at this time become alarmed about being taken up by my old master in Savannah. I was often recognized by students and others from the South; and my master knew where I was. I thought if I went back in the country, if I was taken up I should have more chance to buy myself free; I therefore returned to Litchfield.

After I returned to Litchfield, Mr. Thompson[97] came on as I anticipated, with power from my Master to free me or take me back. He said he would put me in irons; and send me down to New York, and then on to Savannah, if I did not buy myself. I instantly offered to give up my house and land, all I had. The house was under a mortgage to Dr. Cottin. A Mr. Burrows[98] from the South had before this seen me in New Haven, and said my master would send on for me. I got a gentleman in Litchfield to write to my master, to know what he would do, and he wrote back he would take five hundred dollars for me, though I was worth eight. Mr. Thompson had now come on with discretionary power. My house would sell for only $425, under the incumbrance. Mr. T.[99] wished me to give my note for fifty dollars in addition. I went to the Governor[100] and

96. A small community five miles northwest of New Haven.
97. William H. Thompson, originally from Litchfield, was a merchant from Savannah, who acted as Welman's emissary designated to secure payment from Grimes for his freedom.
98. This is likely Benjamin Burroughs, partner of Oliver Sturges.
99. William H. Thompson.
100. Oliver Wolcott, Jr., governor of Connecticut, 1817–1827.

told him the whole story; and the Governor said, not so, Grimes; you must have what you get hereafter, for yourself. The Governor did pity my case, and was willing to assist me, for such is his feeling to the poor.

To be put in irons and dragged back to a state of slavery, and either leave my wife and children in the street, or take them into servitude, was a situation in which my soul now shudders at the thought of having been placed. It would have exhibited an awful spectacle of the conduct and inconsistency of men, to have done it; yet I was undoubtedly the lawful property of my master, according to the laws of the country, and though many would justify him, perhaps aid in taking me back, yet if there is any man in God's whole creation, who will say, with respect to himself, (only bring the case home,) that there are any possible circumstances in which it is just that he should be at the capricious disposal of a fellow being, if he will say, that nature within him, that feeling, that reason tells him so, or can convince him so, that man lies! The soul of man cannot be made to feel it, to think it, to own it, or believe it. I may give my life for the good or the safety of others. But no law, no consequences, not the lives of millions, can authorize them to take my life or liberty from me while innocent of any crime.

I have to thank my master, however, that he took what I had, and freed me. I gave a deed of my house to a gentleman in Litchfield. He paid the money for it to Mr. T., who then gave me my free papers. Oh! how my heart did rejoice and thank God. From what anxiety, what pain and heartache did it relieve me! For even though I might have fared better the rest of life under my master, yet the thought of being snatched up and taken back, was awful. Accustomed as I had been to freedom for years, the miseries of slavery which I had felt, and knew, and tasted, were presented to my mind in no faint image.

To say that a man is better off in one situation than another, if in the one he is better clothed and better fed, and has less care than in the other, is false. It is true, if you regard him as a brute, as destitute of the feelings of human nature. But I will not speak on the subject more. Those slaves who have kind masters are, perhaps, as happy as the generality of mankind. They are not aware that their condition can be better, and I don't know as it can: indeed it cannot, except by their own exertions.

I would advise no slave to leave his master. If he runs away, he is most sure to be taken: if he is not, he will ever be in the apprehension of it;

and I do think there is no inducement for a slave to leave his master and be set free in the Northern States. I have had to work hard; I have been often cheated, insulted, abused and injured; yet a black man, if he will be industrious and honest, can get along here as well as anyone who is poor and in a situation to be imposed on. I have been very unfortunate in life in this respect.

Notwithstanding all my struggles, and sufferings, and injuries, I have been an honest man. There is no one who can come forward and say he knows anything against Grimes. This I know, that I have been punished for being suspected of things of which some of those who were loudest against me were actually guilty. The practice of warning poor people out of town is very cruel. It may be necessary that towns should have that power, otherwise some might be overrun with paupers. But it is mighty apt to be abused. A poor man just gets agoing in business, and is then warned to depart; perhaps he has a family, and don't know where to go, or what to do. I am a poor man, and ignorant; but I am a man of sense. I have seen them contributing at church for the heathen, to build churches, and send preachers to them, yet there was no place where I could get a seat in the church. I knew in New Haven indians and negroes, come from a great many thousand miles, sent to be educated, while there were people I knew in the town cold and hungry, and ignorant. They have kind of societies to make clothes for those who, they say, go naked in their own countries. The ladies sometimes do this at one end of a town, while their fathers, who may happen to be selectmen, may be warning a poor man and his family out at the other end, for fear they may have to be buried at the town expense. It sounds rather strange upon a man's ear who feels that he is friendless and abused in society, to hear so many speeches about charity; for I was always inclined to be observing.

I have forebore to mention names in my history where it might give the least pain; in this I have made it less interesting, and injured myself.

I may sometimes be a little mistaken, as I have to write from memory, and there is a great deal I have omitted from want of recollection at the time of writing. I cannot speak as I feel on some subjects. If those who read my history think I have not led a life of trial, I have failed to give a correct representation. I think I must be forty years of age, but don't know; I could not tell my wife my age. I have learned to read and write pretty well; if I had an opportunity I could learn very fast. My wife has had a tolerable good education, which has been a help to me.

I hope some will buy my books from charity; but I am no beggar. I am now entirely destitute of property; where and how I shall live I don't know; where and how I shall die I don't know; but I hope I may be prepared. If it were not for the stripes on my back which were made while I was a slave, I would in my will leave my skin as a legacy to the government, desiring that it might be taken off and made into parchment, and then bind the constitution of glorious, happy and *free* America. Let the skin of an American slave bind the charter of American liberty!

WILLIAM GRIMES.

Conclusion

IT is now more than thirty years since the foregoing true and eventful Life was written and published. Although a large edition was printed, a very few copies are now in existence; and it was only when I advertised in the public papers, that I was myself enabled to procure a perfect one. By the kindness of a gentleman, who will long be held in grateful remembrance, a copy was put in my hands. A large number of my intimate friends have urgently requested me to print another edition of my Life, with such additions as I can find time to add in this my old age. I am greatly indebted to many distinguished men of New Haven, and the obligations I owe them, I hope in a measure to repay, by presenting to them this second edition of the Life of one who has often been called one of the most remarkable personages of modern times. I comply with the request, for the purpose, in the first place, of raising, if possible, a small amount of money, for I believe almost everybody will purchase a copy of my Life; and in the second place, to gratify the laudable curiosity which so many of my friends have exhibited to procure a true and perfect Life of "Old Grimes."

In presenting this account to my fellow citizens of New Haven, "and the rest of mankind," I do not think it necessary to enter into all the particulars of my life since I have lived in New Haven, as, after a residence here of nearly thirty years, I have become, as the newspapers say, "a fixed institution," and have also become pretty generally known. I shall therefore add but little to the preceding account of one who has tasted the bitter dregs of slavery—having been the slave of *ten* masters— but who has yet been permitted, through a kind Providence, to drink at the fountain of Liberty, although many of his best years were spent in degradation and misery.

I am now an old man—"Old Grimes"—being more than seventy years of age, and the father of eighteen lovely and beautiful children, of whom only twelve, I believe, are living. The youngest child, now eight years old, a smart and active lad, is the only one now with me. The other children that are living are scattered all over the world, one son being now in Australia, digging for gold.

My wife, who at the time we were married, was called in the papers, "the lovely and all-accomplished Miss Clarissa Cæsar," has also grown old, since introduced her to the reader, as may well be supposed; but she is yet very smart, for so fruitful a vine, and I don't think there are many to be compared to her. Like her noble son, she too is seeking for gold, having been for some time in California.[101]

But I must now give my readers a short account of myself from the time I left them in the first part of my book. I then lived in Litchfield, but since that time have lived in a great many places, some of which I will mention. When I left Litchfield, I went with my family to Bridgeport,[102] and set up a barber shop. I was called a good barber, and had a great many customers. I made money quite fast, and ought to gave been satisfied; but somehow I was not, and had to be on the move. So I pulled up stakes, packed up my things, and off we started for Stratford.[103]

But here I should tell what a narrow escape I had from drowning, while I lived in Bridgeport. There was a camp meeting at Saugatuck, and being a good Methodist, I thought I would attend. About five hundred persons got on board the steamboat Lafayette, at Bridgeport, but before we arrived at the camp ground there came up a most dreadful storm of rain, and the wind blew like a hurricane. All the people were almost frightened to death, and expected that the steamboat would sink, and all go to the bottom of the Sound. I never was so scared before, and never expected to feel so awful as I did then; but I came very near being drowned after that time, when I lived in New Haven,

101. San Francisco ship passenger lists suggest that Clarissa Grimes, along with a daughter and son-in-law, may have sailed on the *Winfield Scott* from New York via Panama and Acapulco to San Francisco, arriving on April 28, 1852. Although Clarissa lived in San Francisco for many years, city directory addresses in both San Francisco and New Haven show that she and her children traveled freely between the two cities. The California Grimeses maintained their ties to William Grimes. After Clarissa's death in San Francisco in 1869, her body was transported to New Haven, where she was interred with her husband in the Grimes family plot at the historic Grove Street Cemetery.

102. Bridgeport is on the Connecticut coast, twenty miles south of New Haven.

103. Stratford is five miles north of Bridgeport.

which I will tell all about soon. Although all expected to be lost, we were spared, and at last arrived safe at the camp meeting, and had a good time.

I lived in Stratford some time, but didn't make much by the operation of moving, and so went back to Bridgeport, where I stayed a little while and then went to Norwalk.[104] Here I carried on my old business of a barber, and cleaning old clothes, and made out to live very comfortable. But as at this time I happened to get into trouble, I didn't stay in Norwalk. The trouble I got into was, that a large butcher one day insulted me and I knocked him down. I was then younger than I am now, and if anybody meddled with Grimes, he was sure to be punished, if he wasn't stronger and a better man than I was. I did no more than any one would do when abused, but I being a *negro,* as they called me, and the butcher a *white* man, although his skin was a great deal blacker than mine, I was put under $500 bonds. No one would go bail for poor Grimes, so he had to go to jail. I didn't mind that much, as I had before been in such places; but at last I found a friend in Lawyer Fitch Wheeler, of Monroe,[105] and after I had been in jail about a week, he gave bonds for me, and once more I was enjoying my liberty. When the trial came on, the butcher paid the cost of court, and I was discharged. Afterwards I sued the butcher before a Justice in Bridgeport, got my case, and the butcher had to pay one dollar and the costs of court.

From Norwalk I went to Fairfield. Here I did a good business, shaving and powdering my friends Judge Daggett and Lawyer Nathan Smith,[106] when they came there to attend court. Sometimes I made more than three dollars a day. I had a great run of custom—all the first men of Fairfield came to Grimes to have their hair trimmed and to be shaved. I ought to have been contented, but I wasn't, and again was on the move.

104. Norwalk is thirteen miles south of Bridgeport.

105. Monroe, Connecticut, is fourteen miles north of Bridgeport.

106. Nathan Smith (1770–1835), United States senator and prosecuting attorney for New Haven County from 1817 to 1835. Along with Daggett, Smith publicly opposed the development of a "negro college" in New Haven.

When I say I *shaved* my friends, I want my readers to understand what I mean, for I wasn't then in the brokerage business,[107] which I afterwards followed very successfully, and of which I shall speak soon. Being a barber and being a broker, is quite different, and I hope no one will confound the one with the other.

From Fairfield I went on to Stratford Point.[108] I made out tolerable well there, but after I had been in the place about a year, we packed up all our things, put them on board a sloop, and started for New Haven.

When I got to New Haven, I set up a barber shop and clothes cleaning establishment, in Chapel street.[109] I hired my shop of Esquire Daggett, who was always a good friend to Grimes. Chapel street then wasn't much like what it is now. One could then hire a store cheap, now it takes a great deal of money, and if Grimes could hire a shop anywhere, he would have to go to some old place where the gentlemen wouldn't come. When I got to New Haven, I thought I would let my old friends know what I intended to do, so I put an advertisement in the paper, headed with these lines:

> Old Grimes is not dead,
> But you may see him more,
> Cleaning coats and shaving heads,
> Just as before.
>
> Though long old Grimes has slept,
> He only sleeps to wake;
> And those who thought him dead and gone,
> Now laugh at their mistake.

Here I did a good business, shaving for only three cents, and trimming heads cheap. I also cleaned clothes and did almost everything to get

107. Grimes may be referring here to his occupation as a "Lottery Policy Dealer," as is noted in the United States census for the city of New Haven in 1860.

108. Stratford, Connecticut, is sixteen miles south of New Haven, on the Long Island Sound. Stratford Point refers to the lighthouse built in 1822 at the mouth of the Housatonic River.

109. A central commercial street in downtown New Haven.

an honest living. I have worked at the Colleges, and have always been an industrious man, and have endeavored to get an honest living, and if I could not do it one way I have tried another. That my readers may see what a variety of callings I have been engaged in, I here copy the truthful and interesting lines, written by a gentleman of New Haven, who has long been acquainted with me, and whom I have always considered one of my best friends. I don't know whether I ought to give the name of the author of this poem, and therefore I omit to do so; but any one whose curiosity is excited, can learn my friend's name by calling on me.

Old Grimes' Son

Old Grimes' boy lives in our town,
A clever lad is he,—
He's long enough, if cut in half,
To make two men like me.

He has a sort of waggish look,
And cracks a harmless jest;
His clothes are rather worse for wear,
Except his Sunday's best.

He is a man of many parts,
As all who know can tell;
He sometimes reads the list of goods,
And rings the auction bell.

He's kind and lib'ral to the poor,
That is, to number one;
He sometimes saws a load of wood,
And piles it when he's done.

He's always ready for a job—
(When paid)—whate'er you choose;
He's often at the Colleges,
And brushes boots and shoes.

Like honest men, he pays his debts,
No fears has he of duns;

At leisure he prefers to walk,
And when in haste, he runs.

In all his intercourse with folks,
His object is to please;
His pantaloons curve out before,
Just where he bends his knees.

His life was written sometime since,
And many read it through;
He makes a racket when he snores,
As other people do.

When once oppressed he prov'd his blood
Not covered with the yoke;
But now he sports a freeman's cap,
And when it rains, a cloak!

He's drooped beneath the southern skies,
And tread on northern snows;
He's taller by a foot or more,
When standing on his toes.

In Church he credits all that's said,
Whatever preacher rise;
They say he has been seen in tears,
When dust got in his eyes.

A man remarkable as this,
Must sure immortal be,
And more than all, because he is,
Old Grimes' posterity!

After I had been in New Haven several years—I don't know how many, for I can't keep the run of dates—I went into the brokerage business, and have continued it more or less to the present time. I wasn't exactly at the head of the concern, but still I was considered an indispensable part of the establishment, and although I didn't get *rich* by becoming a broker, others made a great deal of money by my exertions. I would often have dreams, and of course I told my friends of them, and then they would greedily seize the lucky numbers, and be *almost* sure to get a prize.

Some people used to say it wasn't right to sell lottery tickets, but as a great many better people than myself sold tickets, I didn't think I was doing wrong.

About this time I joined the Methodist Church, in this city. After I became a broker, some of my brethren thought I wasn't doing right by selling lottery tickets, and they brought me up before the Church, and turned me out. Thus Grimes got into trouble again; but not despairing, I applied to Dr. Croswell,[110] and was confirmed by the Bishop, and I am now a member in full communion in Dr. Croswell's Church. There were a great many confirmed when I was. While the Bishop put only one hand on the heads of the others, I being the last, he put both hands on mine—thus doubly blessing me.

I now sometimes attend Dr. Stiles' Church,[111] because the Doctor is an old friend of mine. When the Doctor was a student I used to work for him—make his fires and sometimes shave him and dress his hair; and when he went to Litchfield to study law, I also was there, and waited on him.

And now I ought to tell about the other narrow escape from drowning. I don't know what year it was, but it was the same year that the steamer Lexington was burnt in the Sound,[112] and so many lives lost.[113] That was a dreadful accident; but the danger I was in, was almost equal to those unfortunate beings on board of the Lexington.

At this time I lived over on what is called the Dyke,[114] and there came on a most powerful rain storm, and the water rose so fast that

110. Reverend Harry Croswell (1778–1858) was rector of Trinity Episcopal Church in New Haven from 1815 until his death in 1858. In the early 1840s, the African American population of Trinity, led by Alexander Crummell, left the church to form St. Luke's Episcopal Church. Favoring the move, Croswell offered the use of Trinity's parish property.

111. Probably Savannah native Joseph Clay Stiles (1795–1875), the pastor of South Church in New Haven in 1853.

112. Long Island Sound is an estuary between the coast of Connecticut and Long Island.

113. The steamer Lexington burned and sank in Long Island Sound on January 13, 1840, killing 150 passengers.

114. A likely reference to the "Dyke Causeway," which crossed the mouth of West Creek in New Haven.

before we were aware of it, my house was all surrounded with water, and we found it impossible to escape. The water came into the first story and we went to the second, and from the second to the third, and then it was that we all expected to be drowned. This was in the night. At last I got my head out of the garret window, and with a speaking trumpet, cried out most all night, "Oh for a cannon to wake those sleepy men." Finally I waked up a man, and he went and got Rev. Mr. Jewett's *horse* out of the water, and saved *his* life. He too had a narrow escape, his head being only out of the water. After they had got the horse out, the water began to lower, and in a little time we were all left safe from harm.

Now I might as well tell about that witch that I mentioned in the book, riding me. Some persons think it isn't true, but it is, every word of it, and I might tell a great deal more about it. To convince my readers that it is true I must say that I have heard from my old master, and he says that Frankee is dead. He also says that when he thought Frankee was agoing to die he told her that she had been a good slave, and asked her what he could do for her. He asked her what he should do with her things after she was dead; if she wanted any of them given to any of her fellow slaves. No, massa, said she, I don't care about any body. Bury them all with me. And when she died my old massa dug a trench beside of her grave, and put in everything—bed and bed-clothes, tables, chairs, frying-pan, dishes, &c. &c., and buried them all up with her.

I must mention one thing more. Many years ago I bought a burying ground lot, among the rich folks' lot, and had some of my children buried in it, and now they want to get it away, saying they can't find my land. My land was recorded, but yet the new surveyor says he can't find it, and says that there is not any left after others have got their share. I am a poor man, and perhaps because I am I shall not have a place to put my old worn out body, but I know I bought and paid for a lot in the burying ground.

I have now been in New Haven more than thirty years, and have always meant to be an honest man and deal justly with all. I have always tried to pay my debts and keep out of jail; but I have been in jail twice in New Haven—once because I didn't pay Mr. Bradley for breaking his carriage—amounting to twenty dollars, and once because I hadn't the money to pay two or three dollars for rent. My friends, however, raised the money, and I was again free, and hope to remain so.

I said in the former part of my book, that the poor and friendless are not entirely free from apprehension, even in this land of liberty, and that this could be illustrated if I should give all the particulars of my life since I have been in Connecticut, and that I might do so in a future edition. But on reflection I have concluded not to rake up old affairs, and as all the wrongs which I have met with in my eventful life have no doubt been ordered wisely, I have forgiven all, and hope, if possible, to forget them. But when they are called to mind, I think those persons who have oppressed poor Grimes, should recollect that although his skin is perhaps a little darker than theirs, he yet has the feelings of a man, and knows when he is abused.

And now, as I have brought my narrative to a close, I wish only to add a few lines, to say that I hope all my friends and acquaintances will purchase a copy of my book, and thus help "Old Grimes" to pay the printer, and have a small amount left to carry him safely through the coming year. As before remarked, I am now an old man, and am almost wholly dependent on my acquaintances for the means of support; and while the purchasers of my book benefit me by so doing, I hope and believe they will find themselves abundantly repaid by the perusal of it. The book, as will be seen, is *illustrated* by a likeness of "Old Grimes," engraved by Sanford[115] from a Photograph by Wells, Daguerreian Artist, Nos. 10 and 11, Mitchell's Building.[116] I am indebted to the generosity of Mr. Wells for this likeness of myself, and I here return him my thanks, and would recommend all my readers to visit his rooms, examine his specimens of Photograph and Daguerreotype likenesses, and then have their own taken.

Here I part with my readers. It is not likely that I shall ever again appear before the public as an author. I hope, however, long to enjoy the kind regards of the good people of New Haven, and when this old, weary, worn out body is lain in that place prepared for all living, the silent tear may be dropped for "poor Old Grimes," and his frailties, whatever they be, forgotten. To all I now bid FAREWELL!

115. Lockwood Sanford, wood engraver, conducted business in Room 12 of the Mitchell Building on Chapel Street in New Haven.

116. Henry M. Wells, a daguerreotypist, operated a business in the Mitchell Building on Chapel Street. After Wells created the image of Grimes that appears in his 1855 narrative, Sanford engraved it in wood.

Chronology

1756   Benjamin Grymes, Jr., great-grandson of William Fitzhugh, founder of Eagle's Nest plantation in King George County, born January 2 at Eagle's Nest.

1777   Grymes volunteers for Grayson's Continental Line Regiment and is granted rank of Lieutenant in the American Revolutionary army.

1778   Grymes marries Ann Nicholas on December 22. They have five children: William Fitzhugh Grymes (1780–1830); Lucinda Grymes (1782–1808); Benjamin Grymes III (1785–1828); George Nicholas Grymes (1787–1853); Martha Carter Grymes (1796–1867).

1783   American War of Independence ends.

1784   William Grimes, son of Benjamin Grymes, Jr. and an unknown slave woman, born in King George, Virginia. Grimes's probable owner is Dr. William Gibbons Stuart.
       Gradual emancipation legislation enacted in Connecticut, manumitting slaves born after March 1 once they reach the age of twenty-five.

1787	Benjamin Grymes, Jr. dines with George Washington at Mount Vernon, April 13.
	Federal Constitutional Convention adopts the Constitution of the United States.
1788	Timothy Dwight, President of Yale University, New Haven, Connecticut, purchases Naomi, a slave.
1789	George Washington elected first president of the United States.
1790	Slaves comprise 20 percent of the U.S. population, 40 percent in the South.
1793	Cotton gin invented and manufactured by Eli Whitney in New Haven, Connecticut, increasing demand for slaves in the South.
	United States Congress passes first Fugitive Slave Act.
1794	Benjamin Grymes, Jr. murders Robert Galloway, a Fredericksburg, Virginia, merchant but is acquitted on grounds of insanity.
	William Grimes sold to Colonel William Thornton of Culpepper County, Virginia.
1798	*Narrative of the Life and Adventures of Venture, a Native of Africa* published in New London, Connecticut.
1799	Birth of Clarissa Caesar.
	First escape attempt by William Grimes.
1804	Death of Benjamin Grymes, Jr.
	William Grimes visits his mother in Leedstown on his way to Northumberland County, Virginia, where he works as a house servant for George Thornton, son of Colonel William Thornton.
	Ohio passes first "black laws" restricting rights and movements of free blacks. Many northern states enact similar legislation soon thereafter.
1807	United States outlaws international slave trade after January 1, 1808.
1810	*The Blind African Slave, or Memoirs of Boyrereau Brinch, Nicknamed Jeffrey Brace* published in St. Albans, Vermont.
c.1811	Grimes sold to his fifth master, Mr. A——, who transfers him from Virginia to Savannah, Georgia.

1812   United States declares war on England.

1814   Grimes works in the spring on the captured man-of-war *Epervier* and the brig *James Monroe* in the Savannah, Georgia, harbor. Timothy Caesar and his wife, Trial, admitted to membership in the First Congregational Church of Woodbury, Connecticut.

1815   Grimes escapes from Savannah to New York City on board the cargo ship *Casket*. He travels on foot to New Haven, where he works at a variety of jobs.

1816   Grimes opens a short-lived barber shop in New Bedford, Massachusetts.

1817   In January, Grimes is accused of assaulting Elizabeth Bly in New Bedford. Tried twice, he is acquitted both times.
On August 18, William Grimes and Clarissa Caesar are married in New Haven by Rev. Samuel Merwin.

1818   Frederick Douglass born into slavery in Talbot County (Eastern Shore), Maryland.
Connecticut legislature limits suffrage to white male citizens.

1819   William and Clarissa Grimes move to Litchfield, Connecticut, where he establishes a barber shop.
Grimes buys real estate from celebrated furniture maker Silias E. Cheney.
Grimes convicted of keeping a white woman "of bad character" in his house.

1820   Ninety-seven African Americans still held legally as slaves in Connecticut.
United States census lists Grimes as head of a seven-member household in Litchfield.
Renting his shop in Litchfield, Grimes moves to New Haven to work as a barber, grocer, and furniture merchant.
Missouri Compromise outlaws slavery in plains states of the American Northwest.

1822   Denmark Vesey conspiracy exposed in Charleston, South Carolina.

1823   Francis Harvey Welman, Grimes's final master, demands he pay for his freedom. Correspondence over terms of self-purchase extends through the fall.

1824   In April, Grimes purchases his freedom for $500.

1825 *Life of William Grimes, the Runaway Slave, Written by Himself* published in New York City.

1829 *David Walker's Appeal* published in Boston; George Moses Horton's *The Hope of Liberty* published in Raleigh, North Carolina.

1830 United States census lists Grimes as head of a five-member household residing in New Haven.
First National Negro Convention held in Philadelphia, Pennsylvania.

1831 Nat Turner Rebellion in Southampton County, Virginia.
New Haven town council votes to prohibit the founding of a "Negro college" within its borders.

1832 New England Anti-Slavery Society founded in Boston under the leadership of William Lloyd Garrison.
Boarding school for girls founded by Prudence Crandall, a Quaker teacher, in Canterbury, Connecticut, is closed after the admission of a black student.

1834 Connecticut outlaws free education to African Americans.

1838 Frederick Douglass escapes from slavery.

1840 United States census lists William Grimes as head of an eight-person household in New Haven.

1845 *Narrative of Frederick Douglass, an American Slave, Written by Himself* published in Boston.

1848 Final abolition of slavery in Connecticut.

1849 Gold discovered in California's Sacramento Valley.

1850 Compromise of 1850 brings statehood to California and enacts the most comprehensive Fugitive Slave law in U.S. history.
United States census lists William Grimes as head of a five-person household in New Haven.

1852 Clarissa Caesar Grimes, daughter Cecilia Grimes, and son-in-law W. H. Williams arrive in San Francisco on board the *Winfield Scott*.
Uncle Tom's Cabin, authored by Harriet Beecher Stowe (born in Litchfield, Connecticut, in 1811), published in book form.

1853 William Wells Brown's *Clotel; or, the President's Daughter*, the first African American novel, published in London.

1854 Kansas-Nebraska Act repeals Missouri Compromise.

1855   *Life of William Grimes, the Runaway Slave, Brought Down to the Present Time. Written by Himself* published in New Haven.
My Bondage and My Freedom, Frederick Douglass's second autobiography, published in New York City.

1857   United States Supreme Court rules in Dred Scott decision that African Americans are not citizens.

1859   John Brown and his antislavery followers raid the U.S. arsenal at Harpers Ferry, West Virginia.

1860   United States census lists William Grimes as head of an eight-person household in New Haven. His occupation is listed as lottery dealer.

1861   American Civil War begins.

1862   President Abraham Lincoln issues the Emancipation Proclamation, liberating all slaves held in the Confederate States of America as of January 1, 1863.

1865   Collapse of the Confederacy followed by the assassination of Abraham Lincoln on April 15.
Death of William Grimes on August 21. He is interred in the Grove Street Cemetery across from Yale College.

1867   United States Congress passes first Reconstruction Act, dividing the South into military districts and granting suffrage to black males in the former Confederacy.

1869   Death of Clarissa Caesar Grimes on December 15 in San Francisco. She is interred in New Haven with her husband.

Afterword

Regina E. Mason

The formation of identity is a crisis each of us must go through
on our journey to adulthood.

—Jacque Roethler, "Reading in Color," *African
American Review* (Spring 1998)

I was in fifth grade in the spring of 1971 at St. Augustine School in Oakland when my teacher, Sister Helen Walsh, instructed her students
to prepare an oral report based on their *true* country of origin. Sister
wanted to illustrate that America was the new world and that although
we were all Americans, each one of us had relatively recent or lost ties
to another country.

I had no interest in making an African connection, let alone articu-
lating one to my predominately white classmates. It was enough for
me to be black and proud of it. Like many black kids throughout the
nation, I had affirmed my black pride each time James Brown's *Say It
Loud I'm Black and I'm Proud* flooded the local KDIA airwaves in the summer of 1968. No longer "Negro" or "Colored," as my people had been
classified prior to 1966, I had learned that race and identity were clearly

defined as authentically black or white with no room for gray lines. As for the in-between status my Louisiana-born paternal grandmother, Lena Dauterive Brown, had chosen for herself, it confused the message of race and identity in the seemingly monolithic black community of my youth. "You're not black or white," she told me one day when I was about nine years old, "You're brown!" Clearly my grandmother's message didn't mesh with the overwhelming message in the streets, nor would hers be the only mixed message I'd receive on what black was and what it wasn't.

Immediate family on both my maternal and paternal sides was an ambiguous looking group whose appearances, like those of many black Americans from a mixed heritage in the shadow of slavery, probably left many perplexed about the definition of _who_ is black. Yet, for the most part, we had identified ourselves with the nomenclature of the era.

I knew lots of families who looked like mine; I grew up with their children. It was when my siblings and I were on the exterior of our circle of friends and family that others—usually black kids darker than us—decided we weren't black enough or, in at least one incident, not black at all.

"You're white!" three kids no more than eleven jeered at my brother, my sister, and me through their half-open car window as we sat in Dad's silver and black 1968 Buick Riviera in the parking lot of Mayfair grocery store. We were waiting for our father to return to the car with the pack of Salem cigarettes he had hurried in to buy.

"We're not white! We're black!" we shouted back at their insult. This exchange went back and forth for several minutes until the other kids noticed my father, a tall, slender light-skinned man with a medium-size afro and long sideburns, barreling toward the car. Those kids froze stock-still as Daddy gave them a dirty look before getting in our car and driving off. "Never mind those kids," was all Daddy said to us before changing the subject.

There were messages from white kids too that come to mind that were just as curious as the latter. "You're not _really_ black, you're light brown" a fifth-grade classmate said to me, as if to echo Grandma Lena, as we walked home from school. Several months later this same classmate attacked my so-called light-brown self by calling me "black nigger!" during a tiff we got into on the school yard. "No good white bitch!" I yelled back. (So much for Grandma Lena's in-between status.) Fortunately, these confrontational episodes dealing with race and identity were infrequent, yet nevertheless impressionable and especially formative in the racially divided Black Power era of my youth.

We were kids, for goodness sake, living together in a primarily black and white neighborhood doing kid things like playing kick ball in the street, cruising through the block on our bikes, playing hopscotch, and devouring ice cream cones. Yet we were not uninfluenced by the world outside of our community. I will never forget a sing-song chant coined by Black Panthers that was more hypnotic and alluring than any jump rope rhyme I had ever heard: *The revolution has come, time to pick up the gun. Off the pigs!*

I grew up in North Oakland, a couple miles southeast of the University of California campus in Berkeley where student protests were the norm, particularly on the Vietnam War and the local People's Park. Spirited demonstrations sometimes erupted into mayhem, leading the police to inflict teargas and pepper spray on the crowd. Once my own mother, who worked on the edge of campus, narrowly escaped a near-riot demonstration by tying a wet bandana around her face to protect her nose and mouth from the choking airborne chemicals as she ran to her car. With the unsettling sounds of sirens and an overhead helicopter, she carefully, yet illegally, maneuvered her car to safety by driving the wrong way down a one-way street.

In the opposite direction of my North Oakland neighborhood, toward downtown, was the headquarters of the gun-toting "all power to the people" Black Panthers. I saw— mainly through local news that drew national attention—young black men with bold puffed-out afros beneath the rims of black berets, in their signature black leather jackets, advocating *black power* and *revolution* with the heated intensity of a fire-spitting dragon. As a kid I watched from the sidelines in awe and in fear.

I don't quite remember how long Sister gave us to complete the assignment, but naturally I waited until the last minute. What did I know about Africa other than the stereotypical portrayals I had seen in movies and in the weekly episodes of Tarzan? I had somehow believed (through osmosis?) that Africa was a backward place with which I wanted no association. Perhaps I would have thought differently had

I been taught that Africa's ancient civilizations were just as compelling as any in the world. Perhaps I would have been amazed as a fifth grader to learn that the *motherland* indisputably gave birth to all humankind. But those were the lessons of Basil Davidson, the Africanist, not of a parochial Catholic schooling.

Nevertheless, as simple and as innocent as this assignment on "origins" was intended to be, it made me deeply curious *not* for Africa, but for my American heritage. That evening I asked my mother to tell me about my roots.

After my sister and I had done the dinner dishes, Mom sat on the living room couch with a book of crossword puzzles askew on her lap and told me about my history. She began with thinly remembered sketches of people and places I had vaguely recalled hearing about maybe once before. It was a sketchy history with high points consisting merely of hazy references to family ties in New England, an early history in California, a Shakespearian actress, a coachman to a former California governor. Slavery and the South came up only when the conversation shifted to Mom's grandfather, Grandpa Fuller, who, it was clear, had married into our apparently *free* (as far back as we knew) New England family.

My mother, Janet Turner, said her Grandpa Fuller was a gruff man, with a handlebar mustache, whose sternness she remembered over his gentleness. Mom was nine when he died so she had to glean the scant details of his background from her own mother, Hazel Fuller Harris. Still a child when slavery ended, Grandpa Fuller had been born a slave on a Virginia plantation to a favored house servant and white plantation owner.

This revelation fascinated me for a two reasons. It was the first time I had heard talk of my family's enslaved heritage. As if Grandpa Fuller was an artifact on display in a museum, I was floored to learn that my mother had actually known a former slave. Until then, discussions in my family about slavery and its subsequent forms, Jim Crow and segregation, were used solely to illustrate how blacks in general had been historically disenfranchised in this country. Slavery and Jim Crow were ways to shed light on how race problems of my day stemmed from centuries-old racial discord dating back to when Africans were stolen from their homeland and brought here in chains. But in *my* family the effect of slavery on the lives of my actual, traceable kin had never (as far as I knew) been acknowledged, let alone discussed in any sort of personal way.

I questioned Mom about her grandfather's parentage. She said it wasn't uncommon for white men to sire mulatto children like her grandfather. When I pried deeper, she was careful to explain, as best she could, about the sexual vulnerability of enslaved women. If there had been even a small measure of mutual affection between Grandpa Fuller's mother, the "favored" slave, and his white "privileged" father, the details of the relationship were lost to time.

Other themes surfaced during that night's talk that went beyond merely familial names, places, and occupations. These unavoidable subjects made me squirm, but they pointed nonetheless to an enslaved heritage in my family that had been shrouded in miscegenation. I learned about a strange law that dated back to slavery called the "one-drop rule," which made anyone with a single drop of "black blood" a black person. (Law or not, my paternal grandmother never would have subscribed to it, but I unwittingly had because of what I had been taught.) Mom also hinted at the divisive class distinctions within the slave community that let light skin be preferred over dark skin and gave house servants a higher status than field hands. If this was the kind of favoritism afforded Grandpa Fuller's mother, it was enough to make my head spin.

Had my mother's stories been aligned with America's historical timeline, some of the information she imparted would have taken my breath away. For instance, neither of us knew that our early ties in the Golden State dated to the era of the California gold rush. Unfortunately, whatever inspiring details Mom relayed to me about our family past were overshadowed by the inherent complexities of my newly revealed slave heritage. I suppose I should have been excited to learn that ours was a well-established California family, in which there had once been a Shakespearian performer. But I wasn't thrilled. There were too many gaping holes in the history Mom told, too many formless ancestors. The only person she made real to me was Grandpa Fuller because I suppose he had been real to her.

I kept thinking about the circumstances of Grandpa Fuller's illegitimacy by virtue of a backdoor liaison and the hierarchy within the slave community. I found it repulsive that even in overt oppression, the oppressed themselves found, and were given, the power to oppress one another. It seemed as though all my history amounted to was a sullied enslaved past and lost ties to a backward Africa. Where was the black pride I thought I knew, and what did I have to be proud of?

On the day of the class assignment, when it was my turn to present before the class, I mumbled something insignificant about Africa to my peers and quickly sat down. I was glad to have survived the self-imposed history ordeal and content to return to important kid things like school-yard games and chatty girlfriends. I couldn't foresee the struggle that this assignment had touched off inside of me.

Sensing my misgivings about my history, a few weeks after she and I had our talk about roots, Mom took me to see her first cousin Katherine Webb, keeper of the family's lore. I lovingly called this proud, coppery-colored, God-fearing woman Aunty Katherine. If Mom's talk caused me to ponder the grim truths of an enslaved past from which we were not exempt, it was Aunt Katherine who taught me how we managed to carve out a life for ourselves as we navigated an often-stifling America.

Aunty Katherine said we were not of the bottom rung of menial America. Our men had earned and held some of the best jobs a *Colored* could have at the time. She added to what Mom had said about our southern progenitor, Grandpa Fuller. This former slave had become a coachman in the employ of former governor Leland Stanford (so the lore went) and a doorman at the world-class Palace Hotel in San Francisco.

Aunt Katherine confirmed that Grandpa Fuller had been tight-lipped about his background but that a celebrated New England genealogy had revealed his wife, Mary Angeline Williams, born in San Francisco of a California pioneer. Aunt Katherine was sure that Mary Angeline's mother, Cecelia Victoria Williams, Mom's and Aunt Katherine's great-grandmother, had come from New Haven, Connecticut.

As she talked about our roots, Aunt Katherine's normal demeanor became somewhat smug in a quiet yet noticeable way. The more she spoke about our North Eastern ancestors the haughtier she became. Although she said it was a privilege to be from the North rather than from the South, I could hardly understand why. Years later I attributed to her northern bias everything we were led to believe about the

North: that it was the home of the abolitionist movement and the Underground Railroad, and was, for blacks in general, *old freedom* (via the Revolutionary War) rather than *new freedom* (via the Civil War and general emancipation).

Our family's arrival in California was a favorite theme of my aunt. She recalled for me the arduous journey Cecelia Victoria Williams endured aboard a vessel that sailed from New Haven, Connecticut, around the Horn of South America to San Francisco. Apparently Cecelia and her husband, a Mr. Williams, did fairly well for themselves in San Francisco. According to Aunt Katherine, my great-great-grandmother became a lauded Shakespearean actress (just as Mom had said), while her husband, a contractor, built homes throughout San Francisco and Daly City.

Without a doubt, Cecelia's memory has remained firmly planted in the minds of relatives who could not have possibly known her—including Aunt Katherine. This blind affinity perplexed me. Who was this woman, I wondered years later, who still, decades after her death, commanded such reverence and respect by elders, including my own mother, who were either babies or not even born when she died? We had no pictures to speak of, no playbills or programs, only an oral fable. Yet, Cecelia's legacy—whatever it was—had endured down to my time.

As Aunty Katherine reminisced, fragments of family lore emerged that stuck in my memory. One dimly remembered yarn about a male ancestor captured my attention, maybe because my aunt knew only three concrete things about him: that his last name was Grimes, that he was from New Haven, Connecticut, and that he, in some unknown way, had a connection with the Underground Railroad, the clandestine network that helped fugitive slaves reach freedom in the northern states and Canada. Aside from having just studied it in school, I inwardly rejoiced at my ancestor's association with the Underground Railroad because it showed that at least he had been active in his defiance of the cruel system that had oppressed my people.

This Grimes who had defied slavery in some unknown way became my personal hero. As a young person I imagined him to be of historic importance like Frederick Douglass, the only black abolitionist I had ever read about in my grade-school history books. I hungered for more information about Grimes, but my aunt had given me all she knew.

For twenty years I wondered about Grimes and his role in the Underground Railroad, but it wasn't until I had become a wife, in my early thirties, when I was at home raising a toddler and preschooler, that I decided to find out more about my roots and the vaguely known Grimes. Aside from my own personal curiosity, I wanted one day to offer my girls their heritage.

Sometime in October 1991 I took up genealogy as a hobby and soon after began pairing its methods with books on abolition and the Underground Railroad. I was hoping to find mention of a man named Grimes from New Haven with an Underground Railroad connection that might authenticate the family lore—thin as it was. I began my search with a sense of possibility, but after months of dead ends and disappointments, the reality of how big my task was began to set in. Fortunately, just when fruitless frustration tempted me to abandon the silly idea of ever finding Grimes, life unwittingly set me on a fifteen-year course of discovery that would reveal more than I could have ever expected to learn about my most illustrious ancestor.

On a luminous summer afternoon in August of 1992, as my little girls played together, I gathered library books that were due to be returned. I noticed a title that I hadn't read. Taking a seat on my living room couch, I began thumbing through Charles L. Blockson's *The Underground Railroad*. Settling on the chapter *Free New England*, within the first few pages I stumbled upon a passage that made my heart race:

> The Underground Railroad developed in New Haven during the late 1820s.... Among the first fugitives to reach this city via the "freedom road" was William Grimes...from Savannah, Georgia...who escaped that southern city with help from friendly seamen who hid him among bales of cotton. After the vessel landed in New York City, Grimes became connected with Underground Railroad workers who directed him toward Connecticut. Trudging mile after mile through Greenwich and other coastal towns, he finally arrived in New Haven.

Was this the shadowy Grimes Aunt Katherine had spoken of all those years ago? The surname, the city of New Haven, and the mention of the Underground Railroad were telltale signs that made me think he was the same. Blockson's bibliography revealed that William Grimes had written his life story and published it himself in 1855. As I frantically searched for an original edition, a cousin, with whom I shared my find, found an anthology, *Five Black Lives*, at the Oakland Main Library. This compilation, edited by Arna Bontemps in 1971, consisted of five autobiographies written by ex-slaves from Connecticut. Included was the account I had been searching for: *Life of William Grimes, the Runaway Slave, Brought Down to the Present Time*. Cody's Books on Telegraph Avenue in Berkeley had three copies for sale. Following my gut feeling, I bought all three.

As I delved into this man's story, the language astonished me. Unrelenting misery plagued his life, leaving him a profoundly embittered man. Never before had I imagined the depth of the slaves' suffering until I read this man's story. Stripped of property to purchase freedom, Grimes wrote about an unthinkable situation: "Let any one suppose himself a husband and father, possessed of a house, home, and livelihood: a stranger enters that house; before his children, and in fair daylight, puts the chain on his leg, where it remains till the last cent of his property buys from avarice and cruelty, the remnant of a life, whose best years had been spent in misery! Let any one imagine this, and think what I have felt."

Page by page I sifted through this man's 1855 story like an excavator mining for raw gemstones, only my gems of choice were names and places that might ring a bell with Aunt Katherine, the family appraiser.

It pained me to read the circumstances of William Grimes's boyhood. A mother myself, I could hardly stand to imagine the unbearable grief, the utter loss, the sheer helplessness that must have assailed William's mother when her son was sold away at age ten to another master on a far-off plantation.

The slave system that Grimes described had been far more cutthroat than any I could have imagined. He grew up like a wild weed, friendless and motherless, with apparently no surrogate slave family or loved one to embrace him, no one even to look after him, as Fiddler in Alex Haley's *Roots* had cared for the boy Kunta. Struggling alone against harsh masters and crafty slaves, young William learned early the essentials of bare survival within a cruel and indifferent institution. Defenseless, William was repeatedly forced outside the house servants' circle by those obliged to look out first for their own interests. I was numb.

Still in search of some magical clue that might instantly link the past to the present, I dug deeper into Grimes's narrative. It wasn't until I came to the end of the book that I noticed Grimes's wife identified as "the lovely and all accomplished, Clarissa Caesar." Immediately I phoned Aunt Katherine.

"Is Caesar a family name?"

"Hmmm," she thought, searching her mind, "I think it is—but I'm not sure."

Her next comment brought me to my feet. "Oh Gina, I've got to get you the family Bible. All the family names are written in it."

"A Bible?" I exclaimed, "Who has it? Where is it? And why hadn't I heard about this before?"

As a teen I had marveled over my great-grandmother's autograph book, a family heirloom filled with elegant script and philosophical musings from the 1880s, but I had never seen, or so much as vaguely remembered, a family Bible. Neither had my mother. Having grown up hearing about the family Bible, she was convinced that this book was mythical.

But Aunt Katherine was insistent. "Oh, we do have a family Bible," she assured me during another phone conversation, "and when the weather gets better, I'm going to Portland to see if it's tucked away in my sister's attic."

That was fall 1992. Better weather for Aunt Katherine was nearly a year away. Meanwhile I had no choice except to take an alternate long, tedious road to my roots and to perhaps William Grimes—a task that could have been cut in half had I been privy to the names in our family's Bible. I couldn't be sure, however, that there *was* a Bible.

Taking a different route into my family's history, one that a professional genealogist would surely scorn, I decided to look not for *my* family but for *William Grimes's* family. I wanted to see how names in *his* family compared with names in mine, names I had accumulated from censuses in various states, vital statistics, and other records before I had found mention of William Grimes in Blockson's book. The adrenaline boost I needed to sustain me through this search appeared in my mailbox late October.

The Lynn Funeral Home in Tacoma, Washington, informed me that my great- great-grandmother, the Shakespearian actress Cecelia Victoria Watson (Watson was the name of her second husband), had "died of acute bronchitis on September 2, 1920 at eighty-one years of age." Under "Father's Name" on a small index card "Grimes, U.S.A." had been typed. I literally jumped for joy! No longer was the Grimes surname a mere conjecture, but one truly linked to my family line. A big question still remained, however. Was my great-great-great-grandfather just another Grimes or was he the William Grimes who escaped from slavery and published his autobiography in 1855?

I began my search for William Grimes with the 1850 federal census in so-called free Connecticut because I learned that this was the first national census to name each and every individual in a given household. Based on Cecelia's death notice, she would have been eleven years old in 1850. If she was indeed William Grimes's daughter, surely her name should appear in his household around more or less the same age.

The very next morning, I drove up to the Family History Center on the grounds of the Mormon Temple, high in the hills of Oakland, where family names and histories unfolded in microfilm and microfiche and in books and periodicals. I was no stranger to this place; visits to its data collections had now become routine.

After establishing which film to peruse, I settled into a cubical with a reader and began reeling to the page I intended. Through sheets of script that varied from elegant loops to hurried scribbles, true to my hunch, I happened on the name William Grimes, the man I now knew had authored a pioneering fugitive slave narrative. In 1850 he was living in the city of New Haven and county of New London with a total of five in his household. I found two other names along with William's name—Clarissa, his wife, and Tryal Caesar, his mother-in-law. But to my utter shock and disappointment there was no one in the household named Cecelia!

Since the U.S. censuses are taken every ten years, my next option was to search the 1860 census. This time I found eight in the household of an aged William Grimes, but not one name crossed referenced with my family tree. By 1870, William Grimes had either died or vanished.

There were days when I knew with conviction that I had been trailing the right family lines. Sometimes, however, doubt made me think that I had been wasting my time—if not my life—on this project. Like a bad dream I'd sometimes think that I'd been trailing the wrong family and that even if it was the right family, it would be next to impossible to make a lineal connection—especially one conceived over two hundred years ago. There were times, too, when I wasn't so sure I wanted to claim Grimes as my own. His was a bizarre, unfathomable world I could hardly comprehend. A highly superstitious man, he believed in witchcraft, convinced that he had been haunted by a slave witch. He often sought out soothsayers for a preview of his fate. The pages of his book reeked of blood and gore from knock-down-drag-out fights he had engaged in with other slaves. What's more, he had been subjected to terrible violence at the hands of the most perverse slave drivers. He seemed to be a broken soul, psychologically wounded by a viciously oppressive system. Nonetheless I dug deeper, hoping to reach the core of this rebellious slave's life.

Naive about the structure and function of the slave narrative, I turned to the works of scholars to discern even a basic understanding of this unusual genre of literature. I needed someone or at least a body of text to help me make sense of William Grimes. Years before I had even heard of this runaway slave, I had devoured two other slave narratives that were the crème de la crème of their kind: *My Bondage and My Freedom* by Frederick Douglass and *Incidents in the Life of a Slave Girl* by Harriet A. Jacobs. But neither of their works prepared me for that of William Grimes. In fact, nothing I had ever read on slavery had prepared me for the explosive text authored by Grimes.

Through the experts I learned that Grimes had actually published two narratives during his life, first in 1825 and a somewhat expanded version of the same book in 1855. Titles such as *The Slave Narrative Its Place in American History* by Marion Wilson Starling and *The Slave's Narrative* edited by Charles T. Davis and Henry Louis Gates, Jr. helped me grasp a basic understanding of the slave narratives; but in my attempt to make sense of the seemingly unique William Grimes, the work of two noted scholars surfaced: the 1951 article "The Case of William Grimes" by Charles H. Nichols and the1986 book *To Tell A Free Story* by William L. Andrews. No other academics had undertaken an in-depth critique of this ex-slave. These two scholars—as if Grimes's text had been a lab specimen—dissected his words and his psyche, in ways that were mostly true but lacked the compassion I had developed for Grimes. I could not have imagined that in time one of these scholars would challenge me to dig deeper and strive higher in my pursuit of William Grimes.

Cecelia Victoria's whereabouts continued to perplex me to the point of my wondering if she really had a connection to William Grimes. Still I couldn't completely give up on finding her. Maybe she had been living with a relative when the census-taker came around in 1850. After all, when Grimes published his second book in 1855, he claimed to have had at least twelve children still alive. Surely a few of them were adults and on their own. But without the names of the older siblings, a search was pointless. Besides, by the 1860 census, Cecelia Victoria would have been twenty-one years old, old enough to marry. Without her husband's full name or information about where they lived, I had no basis for a search—just fragmented pieces of oral history riddled with holes.

A more fruitful and intriguing alternative beckoned. I had long been curious about the identity of Grimes's white father, the wealthy planter who, according to Grimes's own narrative, shot a "Mr. Gallava" dead on his plantation. Could I identify and locate this violent Virginia slaveholder? My first thought was to pour over microfilms of old newspapers of the region—a daunting task that could have taken months if not years to sort through. But one day I got lucky. The card catalog at Sutro Library in San Francisco directed me to an interesting title: *Genealogical Abstracts from 18th Century Virginia Newspapers* by Robert Headley, Jr. I scooped it up with several other books and headed to the checkout desk. My intent was to thumb through this book as my husband, Brandon, drove us home across the San Francisco Bay. No sooner had we gone a few blocks beyond the Stonestown Galleria shopping mall when an adrenaline rush washed over me. Two citations emerged that corroborated William's story. The second one made me gasp aloud:

"GALLOWAY, Robert, merchant of Fredericksburg, shot and killed by Benjamin GRYMES of Eagle's Nest, King George County...on Friday morning."

Although I was no closer to establishing Grimes as my forbear, I now knew that his autobiography might very well yield up more historical truths that I could document. The murder of Robert Galloway led me to peruse the *Virginia Herald and Fredericksburg Advertiser* of August 7, 1794. Aside from the usual microfilms and readers, both of the genealogical repositories I frequented in the early days of my search carried rows and rows of the histories of "ancient" or "first" families of every region of the United States. I often went searching for the Grimes surname in King George County, Virginia, where I had already noted the older English spelling G-R-Y-M-E-S before I had found the citation that led to William's father. Soon I discovered more about Benjamin Grymes and his plantation, Eagle's Nest.

In 1963, during the height of the Civil Rights movement, a prominent literary and cultural historian of the South, Richard Beale Davis, edited a volume of letters and other documents pertaining to Benjamin Grymes's third maternal grandfather, William Fitzhugh, the founder of Eagle's Nest. Studying *William Fitzhugh and His Chesapeake World, 1676–1701* helped me begin to understand the makings of an early American slaveholding dynasty.

In the late seventeenth century William Fitzhugh was one of the wealthiest men in Virginia. By 1686 he had built Eagle's Nest, "a mile north of the Potomac River, the old highway to England."[1] He was first and foremost a highly respected lawyer, well established in America's oldest legislative body, the Virginia House of Burgesses. Aside from marrying well, he built a fortune as both lawyer and tobacco planter long before cotton became king in the South. When he died in 1701 at age fifty, he left his heirs a fortune comprising well over fifty-four thousand acres of land and assured social access to other influential families of remarkable stature, such as the Revolutionary War–famed Lees and the founding father Washington.

Although Benjamin Grymes was the beneficiary of his ancestor's fortunes, he appears to have been an arrogant fellow with no real course of his own to blaze. Instead, generational inheritance and family name were his main assets. According to Liza Lawrence, author of *The Vista at Eagle's Nest,* and also the last family member to live in the estate, Ben Grymes was at least an imposing physical specimen with a yen for combat: "Benjamin Grymes, Jr. 'five-feet ten inches tall, handsome and well-made' volunteered for Grayson's Continental Line Regiment in January, 1777. He was granted the rank of Lieutenant. Soon after, he was selected for General George Washington's Life Guards."

Apparently Ben Grymes had known George Washington all his life and had proved very competent during his military tenure. However, life as a peaceful and proper gentleman seems to have been more than he could manage. Whether through recklessness or lawlessness, after killing Galloway, Grymes ordered his slaves to throw the murdered man's body into a ditch. Then the defiant master armed his bondmen for battle. Fearless but not suicidal, Grymes refused to give himself up until a military force arrived. On May 8, 1795, Benjamin Grymes was found not guilty for the murder of Robert Galloway on grounds of insanity. He died at home at Eagle's Nest on February 13, 1804.

Eventually the plantation, over two thousand acres vast, was subdivided for the benefit of Benjamin's three white sons—William, Benjamin, and George. The descendants of the Fitzhugh-Grymes clan remained heirs of the Eagle's Nest estate for about three hundred years until Liza Lawrence fell upon hard times and sold the family seat to outsiders in 1974, the year I entered my freshman year in high school. Certainly fate's wheel spun a much different tale for the mulatto slave William Grimes.

On the one hand, it was relatively easy to find the details of William Grimes's white progenitors, their musings and goings on, their successes and their failures, their religious affiliations, their marriages, births, and deaths, their lauded ties to nobility, even what they did for recreation. On the other hand, the only time a slave was mentioned was in reference to a sale or inventory in which he or she was listed among the livestock, dishes, and wares or when he or she was bequeathed to a family member. I found myself growing increasingly edgy, resentful, and even angry at the way slaves were historically obliterated from the white man's memory and life records. Too, while I dug more deeply into the lives of the white Grymeses and Fitzhughs, I remained at a stalemate with the mulatto Grimes, unable to move forward into his genealogy.

The timing could not have been better when my mother phoned to announce that Aunt Katherine was en route home from Portland, Oregon, with important pages she had found tucked inside the family Bible. I was floored. So engrossed was I in my search that I had forgotten my aunt's promise to me nearly one year before.

My dear aunt never liked to fly. The long airy forward motion of the train was her preference, but it was agonizing for me because I wanted her home so that I could see the pages she found in her sister's attic in Portland, Oregon. It was Memorial Day weekend of 1993, and a family barbeque was fittingly planned in honor of her fruitful homecoming.

I was the first to study the aging pages that had, over the years, completely separated from the original spine of the book. As generations of names stared back at me, the awe of the moment struck me in such a way I could hardly speak. For in my hands, on paper so fragile and crumbly, blotted and stained, I held a large piece of my heritage. Someone—some dear one—felt the utmost importance of painstakingly recording each name and each date of significance. Who would have been so bold and so wise as to lay claim to such a legacy worthy of preservation and remembrance? For the first time in my life I felt like I had roots. Not just spindly roots—easily upturned—but anchored roots as solid as the mighty Redwood tree. In all, there were two front and back pages of script spilling to the edges where portions of names and dates had crumbled to dust.

As my eyes skimmed the frail pages, I came across a host of names, many familiar; many unknown. There were the Fullers, the Williamses, the Caesars, and the Grimeses. As I skimmed further down the page, there was the name William Grimes followed by a death date of August 21, 1865. Undeniably, William Grimes—author of the first fugitive slave narrative published in America—was my great-great-great-grandfather. What's more, Cecelia Victoria was there too. She was not only Mom's and Aunt Katherine's great-grandmother, from whom all California and Pacific Northwest relatives stemmed, but William and Clarissa Grimes's daughter too!

Late into the night, after my family and I arrived home from the festivities and had gone to bed, I could not sleep. The culmination of where my journey had taken me thus far and the magnitude of the day fell upon me; I could do nothing but weep. I felt as though the souls of my people had reached across time and generations and were urging me to tell their stories. Then I realized that finding Grimes was not the end of a glorious and at times painful search; it was the beginning. Now, with pages from our Bible, I had more lives to unravel and more tangled roots to untwine—a quest that would take many more years out of my life and carry me thousands of miles away from home.

After that glorious Memorial Day weekend, and with several more years of research under my belt, in June 1998, several family members and I sojourned to Litchfield and New Haven, Connecticut. A year earlier I had connected with Catherine Fields, director of the Litchfield Historical Society. She and her staff graciously arranged for a family reunion to be held in our honor. In New Haven, we made a tearful discovery of the Grimes family plot in the historic Grove Street Cemetery.

We also visited the Whitney Library in New Haven where curator James Campbell invited us to see and touch for the very first time our forebear's 1855 publication. If that wasn't amazing enough, at Yale University I touched, through white cotton gloves, the 1825 version of my forebear's book. Our visit East drummed up the kind of favorable attention "Old Grimes" would have enjoyed.

In the fall of 1999, Aunt Katherine's health began to wane, but she was pleased to learn how her beloved Cecelia, the western pioneer and Shakespearian actress, had arrived in San Francisco with other family more than likely in April 1852. Cecelia had joined a growing group of eastern blacks who brought to California their Yankee mores and enterprise. Collectively, these Easterners started businesses, churches, schools, and libraries of their own and literary societies and newspapers. Many joined forces to become California's first advocates for civil rights.

A few months after the new millennium, my mother and I journeyed to Eagle's Nest in Virginia's Northern Neck, home of Benjamin Grymes and the Fitzhugh legacy. Although the owners of the estate were very gracious to us, I later learned that many of the board members of the local historical society, to whom (I was told) I am (awkwardly) related, were unwilling to accept the legacy of William Grimes as part of the region's multiethnic history. Unfortunately, they were still wedded to half truths—all the more reason to awaken them to the undreamt histories of my ancestors.

The signatures in the family's nineteenth-century autograph book proved to be an additional resource as I worked with a variety of sources to piece together a remarkable bicoastal tale of two cities. Out of New Haven and San Francisco emerged a rich and colorful coterie of black movers and shakers about whom little has been written.

By October 1999, I had returned to my former place of employment, the University of California at Berkeley. Going back allowed me to tap into resources that would take my research to new heights. Magnificent libraries that I would not have ordinarily been privy to were at my disposal, as were special collections, interlibrary loan, and old and rare newspapers. Oh, those glorious newspapers—particularly the black press!

On a day so warm, it was stifling, I retreated to the cool, dark, windowless, Newspaper and Periodical Room within the Charles Franklin Doe Library. I had mapped out my strategy to find Cecelia a couple of days before in an effort to maximize my full lunch hour. There, reeling through the *San Francisco Pacific Appeal*, a black newspaper servicing California and the Pacific Northwest, I happened on an announcement that read:

PLATT'S HALL
MONDAY, EVENING, DEC. 17TH, 1877
MRS. C. V. WILLIAMS
And her
COLORED DRAMATIC TROUPE
Will present the celebrated tragedy, in five acts of
EVADNE
-Or-
THE STATUES

This magnificent find was the first of several I'd gather on the ambitious Cecelia, a woman who, at a time when black women were relegated to the most menial tasks, boldly carved out her own path to become a "celebrated tragedienne." She was alternately known in the black press as *Mrs. Cecelia Williams* and *Mrs. C. V. Williams*.

So much to tell my sweet Aunty Katherine, but, by this time, fading health and dementia prevented her from marveling at the harvest she had sowed so long ago in the spring of 1971 when I was in the fifth grade. We memorialized our beloved matriarch at St. Cuthbert Episcopal Church in Oakland on December 7, 2002. She was eighty-five. I was touched when Marilyn, Aunt Katherine's daughter, asked me to speak at her mother's memorial. It was the least I could do for the aunt who had given me so much.

In search of a metaphor or a quotation that would represent what my dear aunt had given all of us, I happened on a statement by the French philosopher Simone Weil that summed up what Aunt Katherine apparently had long believed: "To be rooted is perhaps the most important and least recognized need of the human soul."

For thirty-six years, Aunt Katherine and Uncle Willie's upper Ney Avenue, East Oakland home was the hub of family gatherings, where she invariably gave lessons in family lore. She was our anchor, our matriarch, whose door was always open. It was in her home that I, a young girl, in the era of black power, black beauty, and black pride, struggled to understand my place in light of competing ideologies of race and identity.

The catalyst for my search had been Sister Helen Walsh's fifth-grade class assignment on one's country of origin. As innocent as the assignment was intended to be, it challenged the very foundation my so-called black pride stood on. Mine was a shallow superficial pride, which was all it could have been at the time. I hadn't lived long enough to know the depth or the measure of what constituted black pride. It was popular to be black. It was popular to chant, "Say it loud, I'm Black and I'm proud," just as it was popular to wear bell-bottoms, hip-huggers, or windowpane jeans. The black pride I knew lacked the depth, the emotional profundity, the wisdom and richness gleaned from the collective black experience coupled with the pride culled from a remarkable family history. Indeed, I am wiser for this journey and more complete as a person.

As my quest for roots continues to take me deeper into the past, I no longer dismiss Africa as I did in fifth grade. The memory of my earliest known black progenitor, Timothy Caesar (father-in-law of William Grimes), born around 1742, won't let me, nor do I want to. While I am intrigued by the mystery that this man's history presents, I don't romanticize an Edenic homeland in Africa absent her own role in the transatlantic slave trade.

If the catalyst for this quest was the class assignment, the pulse of the journey came from the once-shadowy Grimes of family lore. So much of what has reached across time to me about William Grimes has been painful, unbearably painful in many respects, but I don't dwell there. To do so would place me in danger of losing sight of his accomplishments. That he penned the first fugitive slave narrative published in America is a remarkable feat. Even more inspiring to me, however, is the way in which he succeeded against almost insurmountable odds to write his story and then to get it published. If there is one thing I have learned from my forefather Grimes, it is to remain true to one's highest ambition, just as he had the audacity to remain true to his.

Regina E. Mason
February 20, 2008

Notes

Introduction

1. The two-volume *Interesting Narrative of the Life of Olaudah Equiano, or Gustavus Vassa, the African* had appeared in London in 1789, but in it the author, Equiano, identifies himself specifically as a black Englishman. Although Equiano's *Life* was a seminal text in the slave narrative tradition in English, Equiano was neither an African American nor a fugitive from slavery. He purchased his freedom lawfully in 1766.

2. Aside from brief comments, the only extensive scholarly or critical discussions of Grimes and his work are: Charles H. Nichols, "The Case of William Grimes, the Runaway Slave," *William and Mary Quarterly,* 3rd ser., 8, no. 4 (October 1951): 552–60; and William L. Andrews, *To Tell a Free Story: The First Century of Afro-American Autobiography, 1760–1865* (Urbana: University of Illinois Press, 1986), 77–81. The 1855 edition of Grimes's *Life* is reprinted in Arna Bontemps, ed., *Five Black Lives* (Middletown, CT: Wesleyan University Press, 1971); and in Yuval Taylor, *I Was Born a Slave, vol.* 1 (Chicago: Lawrence Hill, 1999).

3. "Old Grimes Is Dead," *Daily Palladium* (New Haven, CT), August 21, 1865.

4. For discussions of the situation of African Americans, enslaved and free, in Connecticut and New England generally in the early nineteenth century, see Leon Litwack, *North of Slavery* (Chicago: University of Chicago Press, 1961); Edgar J. McManus, *Black Bondage in the North* (Syracuse, NY: Syracuse University Press, 1973); James Oliver Horton and Lois E. Horton, *In Hope of Liberty* (New York: Oxford University Press, 1997); and Joanne Pope Melish, *Disowning Slavery* (Ithaca, NY: Cornell University Press, 1998). For commentary on Connecticut's response to slavery and its pervasive racism, see McManus, *Black Bondage*, 169–70, 183, 184; Melish, *Disowning Slavery*, 201–4; Hillary F. Moss, "Education's Inequity: Opposition to Black Higher Education in Antebellum Connecticut," *History of Education Quarterly* 46 (March 2006): 33; and Guocon Yang, "From Slavery to Emancipation: The African Americans of Connecticut, 1650s–1820s" (Ph.D. thesis, University of Connecticut, 1999). See also the chronology in this book.

5. Melish, 70.

6. Christopher Malone, "Race Formation, Voting Rights, and Democratization in the Antebellum North," *New Political Science* 27, no. 2 (2005): 181.

7. Across New England the first decades of the nineteenth century saw a wave of regional boosterism that embraced a myth of New England as historically free, white, and republican. As Joanne Pope Melish demonstrates, this myth propagated a popular notion throughout New England of the African American in freedom as so "degraded" and out of place that repatriation outside the United States was the only solution to the region's "Negro problem." See Melish, *Disowning Slavery,* 210–23.

8. See, for instance, *The Life, and Dying Speech of Arthur, a Negro Man* (Boston, 1768); *Last Words and Dying Speech of Edmund Fortis, a Negro Man* (Exeter, Maine, 1796); and *The Life, Last Words and Dying Speech of Stephen Smith* (Boston, 1797). Facing the gallows, Arthur warned slaves "as they regard their own souls, to avoid desertion from their masters" among other sins such as "drunkenness" and "lewdness." Ten African American criminal confession narratives were published before Grimes's 1825 *Life.* The editor of *Sketches of the Life of Joseph Mountain, a Negro Who Was Executed at New-Haven, on the 20th Day of October, 1790, for a Rape, Committed on the 26th Day of May Last* (New Haven, CT: T. and S. Green, 1790), was David Daggett, whom William Grimes mentions in the 1825 edition of the *Life of William Grimes* and calls a "friend" in the 1855 edition. The most famous contributions to the African American criminal confession genre are *The Confessions of Nat Turner,* ed. Thomas R. Gray (Baltimore: T. R. Gray, 1831); and Alex Haley's *The Autobiography of Malcolm X* (New York: Grove, 1965).

9. The "proprietor" and likely author of the *Confession of John Joyce, Alias Davis... with an Address to the Public and People of Colour* (Philadelphia: Bethel Church, 1808) was Rev. Richard Allen, a founder of the African Methodist Episcopal Church. In the address that prefaces Joyce's *Confession*, Allen warns the readers of Joyce's narrative against a variety of transgressions lest they become, like Joyce, "slaves of Sin" and follow him to an ignominious end.

10. The best study of the life of Jeffrey Brace is *The Blind African Slave*, ed. Kari J. Winter (Madison: University of Wisconsin Press, 2004).

11. Ibid., 182.

12. In his useful summary article, "Afro-Americans and Moral Suasion: The Debate in the 1830's" (*Journal of Negro History* 83 [Spring 1998]: 127–42), Tunde Adeleke notes that the moral suasionist argument in American abolitionism had its roots in the reform work of the Society of Friends and in the self-help and cooperative activities of free blacks in the North in the late eighteenth century. Moral suasion as an antislavery strategy rejected more aggressive political (and certainly violent) efforts to extirpate slavery from American soil in favor of a strategy that would overthrow racial prejudice—assumed to be the root cause of slavery—by the power of reason and Christian love. At the heart of the moral suasion philosophy was faith in the efficacy of direct appeals to the moral conscience of slaveholders, indeed, to the entire nation, to produce steady progress toward the ultimate triumph of an enlightened egalitarian spirit in the United States. For the role of moral suasion in the abolitionism of William Lloyd Garrison and his adherents, see James Brewer Stewart, *Holy Warriors* (New York: Hill & Wang, 1996), 51–74.

13. George White, *A Brief Account of the Life, Experience, Travels, and Gospel Labours of George White, an African* (New York: John C. Totten, 1810) in *Black Itinerants of the Gospel: the Narratives of John Jea and George White,* ed. Graham Russell Hodges (Madison, WI: Madison House, 1993), 52–53.

14. White, *Brief Account*, 53.

15. Ibid., 83.

16. Solomon Bayley, *A Narrative of Some Remarkable Incidents in the Life of Solomon Bayley: Formerly a Slave in the State of Delaware, North America. Written by Himself.* ed. Robert Hurnard (London: Harvey and Darton, 1825), 3.

17. A Delaware slave who had been conveyed out of state by his master, Bayley contends in his *Narrative* that on his return to his home state he

had a right to freedom under Delaware law. He made his unlawful escape attempt, he insists, only because his master kidnapped him and jailed him in Virginia to prevent Bayley from bringing suit for his freedom in a Delaware court.

18. Venture Smith, *A Narrative of the Life and Adventures of Venture, a Native of Africa* (New London, CT: C. Holt, 1798), 30.

19. After recounting the purchase of his enslaved wife, Meg, Smith notes that he "purchased a negro man for four hundred dollars. But he having an inclination to return to his old master, I therefore let him go. Shortly after I purchased another negro man for twenty-five pounds, whom I parted with shortly after." Smith later sums up: "Being about forty-six years old, I bought my oldest child Hannah, of Ray Mumford, for forty-four pounds, and she still resided with him. I had already redeemed from slavery, myself, my wife and three children, besides three negro men" (Ibid., 27).

20. Ibid., iii.

21. *The History of Mary Prince* (London: Wesley & Davis, 1831); *The Confessions of Nat Turner* (Baltimore: Thomas R. Gray, 1831); *Narrative of the Adventures and Escape of Moses Roper* (London: Darton, Harvey, and Darton, 1837); *Narrative of the Life of Frederick Douglass* (Boston: American Anti-Slavery Society, 1845); *Narrative of William W. Brown* (Boston: American Anti-Slavery Society, 1847); *Narrative of the Life and Adventures of Henry Bibb* (New York: the Author, 1849); *Narrative of Sojourner Truth* (Boston: the Author, 1850); and Harriet Jacobs's *Incidents in the Life of a Slave Girl* (New York: the Author, 1861)—in short, the most famous African American slave narratives of the antebellum era—bear extensive evidence of the participation of whites as prefacers, editors, recommenders, and publishers. The role of whites in authenticating these texts for a skeptical white reading public has been widely discussed by scholars. See Robert Stepto, "I Rose and Found My Voice: Narration, Authentication, and Authorial Control in Four Slave Narratives," in *From Behind the Veil: A Study of Afro-American Narrative* (Urbana: University of Illinois Press, 1979), 3–31 ; William L. Andrews, *To Tell a Free Story*, chaps. 1–4; and John Sekora, "Black Message/White Envelope: Genre, Authenticity, and Authority in the Antebellum Slave Narrative," *Callaloo* 10, no. 3 (Summer 1987): 482–515. Other than Grimes's *Life*, the only notable antebellum slave narrative to be published with no framing documents by whites is William and Ellen Craft's, *Running a Thousand Miles for Freedom* (London:

William Tweedie, 1860). Embedded within this narrative, however, is an extensive recommendation letter by the Connecticut Unitarian minister and reformer, Samuel May, one of the Crafts' many white sponsors after they made their way to freedom. See *Running a Thousand Miles for Freedom*, ed. John Ernest (Acton, MA: Copley, 2000), 56–61. The publisher of *Running a Thousand Miles for Freedom* was also one of England's most committed white abolitionists.

22. The first African American autobiography to bear the *Written by Himself* subtitle was *The Life, History, and Unparalleled Sufferings of John Jea, the African Preacher. Compiled and Written by Himself* (Portsea, England: the Author, c. 1811). The subtitle is misleading, however, given Jea's comment at the end of his narrative: "I have stated this [his narrative] in the best manner I am able, for I cannot write, therefore it is not quite so correct as if I had been able to have written it myself." The same year in which Grimes's *Life* appeared, Solomon Bayley's *Narrative* also came out bearing the *Written by Himself* subtitle.

23. In 1825, Grimes credited his wife, Clarissa, with "a tolerable good education, which has been a help to me." It is also possible that he attained a degree of literacy as a slave, since one occasion for a rumpus in Savannah arose because of Grimes's having been accused of caricaturing in pencil images and words a physician friend of his master.

24. William Grimes's father was Benjamin Grymes, Jr. (1756–1804), owner of the Eagle's Nest estate in King George County, and was an officer in the Revolutionary army, a prominent planter in Virginia's Northern Neck, and a friend of George Washington.

25. Grimes's recollections of how he successfully masqueraded as a white man in order to deceive the patrols that enforced curfews for slaves in Savannah are the first mentions of passing for white in the African American slave narrative tradition.

26. Consider Grimes's explanation for a tussle he got into in Norwalk, Connecticut: "A large butcher one day insulted me and I knocked him down. I was then younger than I am now, and if anybody meddled with Grimes, he was sure to be punished, if he wasn't stronger and a better man than I was. I did no more than any one would do when abused, but I being a negro, *as they called me*, and the butcher a white man, although his skin was a great deal blacker than mine, I was put under $500 bonds. No one would go bail for poor Grimes, so he had to go to jail" [emphasis added].

27. Frederick Douglass, *Narrative of the Life of Frederick Douglass, An American Slave. Written by Himself*, ed. William L. Andrews and William S. McFeely (New York: W. W. Norton, 1997), 39.

28. See Andrews, *To Tell a Free Story*, 93, 147–48, and 163–64.

29. Moses Roper, *Narrative of the Adventures and Escape of Moses Roper from American Slavery*, in *North Carolina Slave Narratives*, ed. William L. Andrews (Chapel Hill: University of North Carolina Press, 2003), 74.

30. The only instance of Grimes forgiving anyone while he was enslaved occurs on p. 75 when he says that he forgave A. S. Bulloch for accusing him of stealing a bottle of wine. In his 1855 conclusion, as already noted, seventy-one-year-old Grimes states that "I have forgiven all."

31. For a discussion of the expectations of the antislavery movement with regard to the rhetoric of the slave narrative in the late 1830s and 1840s, see Andrews, *To Tell a Free Story*, 97–111. The formulaic character of the slave narrative in the 1840s is reviewed in James Olney's " 'I Was Born': Slave Narratives, Their Status as Autobiography and as Literature," in *The Slave's Narrative*, ed. Charles T. Davis and Henry Louis Gates (New York: Oxford University Press, 1985), 148–75.

32. In his 1845 *Narrative,* Douglass recalls his desperate reliance on conjure—a "root" given him by a fellow slave named Sandy—to protect himself from the vindictive slave breaker, Edward Covey. The root, however, does not prevent Covey from attacking Douglass. In Douglass's second autobiography, *My Bondage and My Freedom* (1855), he identifies Sandy as a "conjurer" and the root as a means of "divination," to which the teenage Douglass had "a positive aversion" because he believed indulging in "the black art" was "sinful" (*My Bondage and My Freedom*, ed. William L. Andrews [Urbana: University of Illinois Press, 1987], 147–48). Nevertheless, as he states in his 1845 account, Douglass acknowledges in his second autobiography that he carried the root as Sandy advised him, though it protected him only one day. After describing his heroic act of self-defense against Covey in their famous hand-to-hand battle, Douglass adds in a footnote, "Sandy would claim my success as the result of the roots which he gave me. This superstition is very common among the more ignorant slaves. A slave seldom dies, but that his death is attributed to trickery" (162). In *Narrative of William W. Brown, a Fugitive Slave* (1847), William Wells Brown admits to having visited a fortune-teller when he was a slave, though now, as he pointedly notes, "I am no believer in soothsaying" (*From Fugitive Slave*

to Free Man: The Autobiographies of William Wells Brown, ed. William L. Andrews [Columbia: University of Missouri Press, 2003], 71). For similar mentions of slave "superstitions" rejected by fugitive slave narrators, see *The Life and Adventures of Henry Bibb, an American Slave*, ed. Charles J. Heglar (Madison: University of Wisconsin Press, 2001), 39; and James W. C. Pennington, *The Fugitive Blacksmith* (London: Charles Gilpin, 1849), 32.

33. Statements of Christian piety such as Douglass's "I love the pure, peaceable, and impartial Christianity of Christ" in the appendix to his 1845 *Narrative* are alien to the *Life of William Grimes*, in which the words "Jesus," "Christ," and "Christian" are totally absent. Henry Bibb spoke for many mid-century slave narrators in stating unequivocally in his *Life and Adventures of Henry Bibb*: "I believe slaveholding to be a sin against God and man under all circumstances" (*The Life and Adventures of Henry Bibb, an American Slave*, ed. Charles J. Heglar [Madison: University of Wisconsin Press, 2001], 204). Grimes does not use the word "sin" in his autobiographies.

34. Unlike his successors in the slave narrative, Grimes never renounces his belief in the demonic powers of sorcery. In the conclusion to his 1855 *Life*, he pauses to "tell about that witch that I mentioned in the book, riding me. Some persons think it isn't true, but it is, every word of it, and I might tell a great deal more about it."

35. In 1825, Grimes did not mention Clarissa Caesar's name in his autobiography. In his 1855 conclusion, however, the "plain looking girl in New Haven" becomes "the lovely and all-accomplished Miss Clarissa Caesar." Grimes quotes from the following marriage notice in the New Haven *Columbian Register* for August 23, 1817: "Married (by particular request) on the 18th Inst. by the Rev. Mr. Merwin, Major William Grimes, Hairdresser (and a distinguished federalist) to the lovely and all accomplished Miss Clarissa Caesar, of New Haven."

Afterword

1. Liza Lawrence, *The Vistas at Eagle's Nest* (Fredericksburg, VA: Fredericksburg Press, 1969), 1.

CPSIA information can be obtained
at www.ICGtesting.com
Printed in the USA
BVHW031548190920
589128BV00002B/8

9 780195 343328